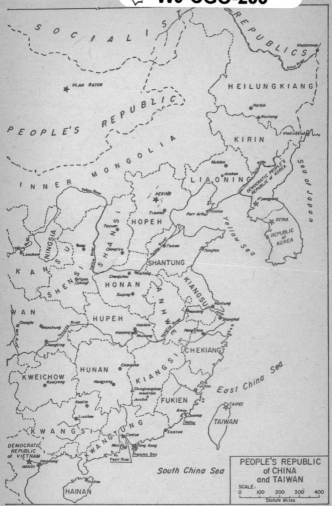

PEOPLE'S REPUBLIC
of CHINA
and TAIWAN

SCALE:
0   100   200   300   400
Statute Miles

JOHN SCOTT was born in Philadelphia, and attended the University of Wisconsin and the Sorbonne in Paris. He has been Assistant to the Publisher and Special Correspondent for *Time Magazine* since 1962. Previously he had been a correspondent and bureau chief for *Time* in many areas of the world, particularly the Far East. During the fall of 1966 he served as visiting professor at the Fletcher School of Law and Diplomacy at Tufts University. Mr. Scott is the author of several books, including EUROPE IN REVOLUTION, POLITICAL WARFARE, and DEMOCRACY IS NOT ENOUGH. He lives with his family in Ridgefield, Connecticut.

The cover design for this edition is by Milton Charles.

CHINA
THE HUNGRY DRAGON

JOHN SCOTT

AN AVON CAMELOT bOOK

AVON BOOKS
A division of
The Hearst Corporation
959 Eighth Avenue
New York, New York 10019

First Printing (Camelot Edition), April, 1969

CAMELOT TRADEMARK REG. U.S. PAT. OFF. AND
FOREIGN COUNTRIES, REGISTERED TRADEMARK—
MARCA REGISTRADA, HECHO EN CHICAGO, U.S.A.

Printed in the U.S.A.

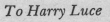

To Harry Luce

CHINA
THE HUNGRY DRAGON

CONTENTS

Introduction to the Camelot Edition . 15

Introduction 21

1. The Land is Large, its History Long . 25

2. A Century of Shame and Humiliation 40

3. The Communists Win 47

4. The Communists Rule 56

5. The Sino-Soviet Conflict 77

6. China's Relations with
   Other Countries 91

7. China's Economy in the Mid-'60s . . 99

8. The Republic of China and Other
   Overseas Chinese 108

9. The Great Cultural Revolution . . 118

10. The Future of China 129

Appendix 138

Biographical Sketches of
Prominent Chinese 152

Brief Bibliography 162

Index 165

ACKNOWLEDGMENTS

To MY FRIEND and former colleague, S. T. Hsieh, a graduate of Yenching University, Peking, now a journalist in Hong Kong, I owe thanks for gathering material on the Chinese economy, arranging interviews for me with Chinese from the Mainland, helping me find my way among the China-watchers in Hong Kong and helping me through their often contradictory reports. Without his cooperation I would have been unable to structure my ideas and formulate them into this book.

To my diligent and dedicated researcher, Julie Thordarson, I owe thanks for invaluable help in preparing this manuscript.

Finally, to Time Inc. I owe thanks for allowing me to use material compiled for my earlier report to the publisher, "Crisis in Communist China."

CHINA
THE HUNGRY DRAGON

INTRODUCTION TO THE CAMELOT EDITION

DURING 1967 AND 1968, Mainland China went through a cataclysmic experience as various groups of Red Guards, the central and regional organs of the Communist Party, the new Revolutionary Committees and the army fought for control of the country. China-watchers in Hong Kong followed the struggle by monitoring central and regional radio broadcasts, by interviewing travelers and refugees from China, by studying newspapers, books, and posters smuggled out and, in some cases, by searching the pockets of the mangled corpses which floated down the Pearl River from Canton. They carefully followed China's imports and exports, flowing in large measure through the port of Hong Kong, and examined the quality and variety of the goods offered for sale by the Chinese in their trade fairs in Canton and abroad.

In this way they pieced together a reasonably accurate though by no means complete picture of what occurred in China. This was accomplished in spite of the fact that during these years the Peking government published no production figures for industry or agriculture, and foreign diplomats in Peking were so restricted in their contacts and movements that their reports were of limited value.

POLITICAL DEVELOPMENTS

Liu Shao-chi had become so isolated and the apparatus of the Party, still in many cases loyal to him, so paralyzed by early 1968 that it ceased to be an effective instrument of political leadership either nationally or regionally. In many cases regional and local party organs held no meetings for months at a time. The local governmental organizations, also at least in part loyal to Liu Shao-chi, were likewise disorganized and unable to discipline the Red Guards who ran rampant through the country "making revolution" and fighting with one another for control of local institutions, factories, communications, and utilities. Most schools and colleges were closed; those in operation concentrated on reciting the thoughts of Chairman Mao, and no serious instruction was carried out.

During the summer of 1968 Chairman Mao, backed by Chiang Ching, Chen Po-ta, Lin Piao, and Chou En-lai began to create Revolutionary Committees under the leadership of the "Proletarian Headquarters" in Peking. By October, 1968, they had succeeded in setting up Revolutionary Committees in all of the country's 21 provinces, five "autonomous" regions, and three direct municipalities.

Mao's original idea was to head each Revolutionary Committee by a troika representing the Party, the army and the Red Guards. This proved impossible, however, because of the violent conflicts among those groups. Mao was forced to depend increasingly on the army, so that by October, 1968, 25 of 29 Revolutionary Committees were headed by military commanders in many cases not completely under the control of the military high command in Peking. But this predominance of the military in the committees ensured support of local military garrisons, thus making possible the reestablishment of some measure of order. The Red Guards were advised to go home, to "learn from the working masses" by doing manual work pending the reorganization of the educational institutions where many of them had studied.

Perhaps the most unkind cut came from their erstwhile champion and patron, Chiang Ching, who told a huge rally in Peking: "You are divorced from the broad masses of the people and from your own units and organizations." At the same gathering Premier Chou En-lai urged the young people to correct their mistakes by "going to the grassroots levels, the production centers, the mountainous areas and border regions, and doing physical work in factories, mines, and villages."

Some Red Guards grumbled at these directives, also at Mao's orders to break the bourgeois intellectuals' domination of China's schools by turning education over to the workers. Such dissenters were shipped off summarily to the boondocks. There they were put to work, along with functionaries of the old Party and government organizations, on land reclamation, construction jobs, and other arduous tasks. After a prolonged period of hard work and plain living these functionaries and hopeful intellectuals might be rehabilitated and allowed to express their boundless love and loyalty to Chairman Mao by returning to political work, or perhaps even to study.

There were indications that Mao and his handful of close associates contemplated an eventual attempt to reform and restructure the Communist Party with the help of these rehabilitated and chastened men and women. But for at least the next several years, the country was to be run by the Revolutionary Committees and the army—all under the leadership of Chairman Mao. Thus, Mao asserted, the Great Cultural Revolution had now done its job. The stamp of finality was put on this assertion by the expulsion in October, 1968, of Liu Shao-chi from the government and the Party by the enlarged twelfth plenary session of the Central Committee under the chairmanship of Mao.

To begin the work of restructuring China, Mao announced that the Ninth Congress of the Communist Party would be held shortly. It was noteworthy that the Eighth Congress had been held in 1956, and, according to the Party statutes, the next should have convened not longer than five years later. But in 1962, the country was shuddering under the failures of the Great Leap, and a congress probably would have repudiated Mao's leadership.

Though the work of reconstituting a new Party and state apparatus was still ahead, Mao and his colleagues could congratulate themselves on the fact that as 1968 drew to a close, relative order had been reestablished, and, thanks to a good harvest the previous year, most Chinese were getting enough food to keep them alive and working.

And, generally speaking, the huge country was still under the centralized leadership of Chairman Mao and Peking.

If two years of the near-chaos of the Great Cultural Revolution had badly shaken China's political structure, its effects on the economy were at least as serious. Industrial production was at least 15 per cent lower in 1967 than in 1966, capital construction dropped by 9 per cent, and crop prospects for 1968 were not bright. It seemed highly unlikely that agricultural production would be anything near the estimated 190 million ton bumper crop of 1967.

To deal briefly with the economy sector by sector: The crop of 1967, probably about equal to the previous all-time record of 193 million tons in 1958, was due partly to generally good weather and partly to the fact that the Great Cultural Revolution had been accompanied by a weakening of Mao's commune-oriented influence in the countryside and the consequent reactivation of more private gardens and farm animals throughout the country. Still another factor probably was the encouragement to the farmers to grow more food because the transportation breakdown had made it more difficult for the state to seize the harvests. But no reliable information is available on these points. It is known that no widespread hunger was reported in any part of China in 1968, and that the country's rice exports were resumed in 1967 to about one million tons (having been far less for several years); and grain imports, mainly wheat from Australia and Canada, were cut back from 6.4 million tons in 1964, to 6 million tons in 1965, to 5.5 million tons in 1966, and finally to 4.3 million tons in 1967.

It is interesting to note that as grain imports were cut back, fertilizer imports were increased; this probably offset the reduction in domestic fertilizer production in the past two years due to shortage of coal and disarray in transport as well as in the fertilizer plants themselves.

Transportation problems, shortages of coal and power, strikes, and other disorders seriously affected industrial production in 1967 and 1968. The estimated overall 15 per cent decline in industrial production in 1967 reversed an upswing of increasing production of the previous five years.

Coal furnishes 90 per cent of China's energy, so that the fall in production in 1967 by roughly 25 per cent—to about 190 million tons—triggered many secondary problems in other industries. Less is known about mining of other minerals. But foreign buyers who have gone to China to place orders for iron ore, tin, tungsten, antimony, flourspar and other concentrates usually exported by China, reported great difficulty in getting both commitments and deliveries.

No quantitative estimates are available on China's petroleum production in 1967 and 1968, but many reports indicate that consumption of both gasoline and diesel oil was severely rationed, and frequently bus and truck transport has been interrupted for lack of fuel.

China's largest manufacturing industry is textiles, and here production was drastically reduced in 1967, often due to factional fighting in the textile mills. Foreign buyers have had consistent difficulty in getting deliveries of textiles, and frequently the meager cloth ration has not been available for Chinese consumers.

Since severe fighting occurred in Anshan and in Wuhan it is not surprising that steel production was off in 1967, probably about 20 per cent lower than in 1966. This was reflected in increases in China's purchases of steel, particularly from Japan.

Little is known about China's military industry. It is interesting, however, that Chou En-lai stated in a January 17, 1968 speech in Peking that the Great Cultural Revolution had interfered with national defense production and with scientific research. During the same period, Chinese shipments of military materiel to North Vietnam and to the Viet Cong were sharply reduced (and compensated for by increases in Soviet deliveries of the same items).

China's exports were seriously affected by the Great Cultural Revolution and fell by 9 per cent in 1967, whereas previously they had been rising for several years. China's imports, on the other hand, have not been affected and actually increased by an estimated 6.5 per cent in 1967 over 1966, creating a trade deficit of some

$250 million in 1967, the largest since 1955. Japan and Hong Kong remain China's top trading partners in spite of reductions in total turnover of 10 per cent and 18 per cent respectively for 1967 over 1966. One reason for the drastic reductions in China's trade with Hong Kong was the disorders in the Crown Colony which grew out of the efforts of Hong Kong Communists to bring the Great Cultural Revolution there.

West Germany replaced the Soviet Union as China's number three trading partner for 1967. Indeed, the Soviet Union fell from third to twelfth place as Sino-Soviet relations worsened. Figures for China's exports for the early months of 1968 indicate a further rapid decline.

The prospects for the immediate future are poor because of the cumulative problems created by breakdowns in transport and reduced production of coal. But the future is, in any case, likely to be seriously influenced by the policies adopted at the Ninth Party Congress—if and when it takes place. It is known that Mao intended to use the Great Cultural Revolution as the springboard into a new Great Leap. This would imply the elimination of incentive bonuses and other "capitalist" instruments in industry and commerce, and the drastic reduction of the private sector in agriculture. Yet it is precisely the use of such incentives and private gardens, along with the army takeover of many factories and farms, that has permitted China to survive the Great Cultural Revolution as successfully as it has.

If Mao now decrees another crackdown in both industry and agriculture, most observers believe that mass insurrection and chaos might follow.

New York
December, 1968.

INTRODUCTION

DURING LATE 1966 and the first months of 1967 while I was writing this book, Mainland China was undergoing a unique civil war. In common with the Soviet Union during the purges of the 1930s, it was a "limited" conflict. Communists were fighting Communists for control of the institutions they themselves had created.

Of course both conflicts were "unlimited" for those killed, Marshal Vasili Blukher and Mikhail Borodin— the Soviet Union's top representatives in China during the 1920s—died as miserable victims of Stalin's manic purges. Chang Lin-chih, Minister of the coal industry of the Peking government, was beaten to death by Red Guards in Peking in late February, 1967. Lo Jui-ching, who had disappeared from his position as chief of staff of the People's Liberation Army in November, 1966, was pictured under torture by Red Guards on Peking posters in February, 1967, and was later reported to have committed suicide.

But in spite of the millions who died, both these conflicts were struggles within Communist leadership groups. They were not "class wars," as were the French Revolution and many Chinese peasant rebellions. The fact that Peking leadership insists on calling the current conflict in China a class war is representative of the inaccuracy of Marxist analyses of recent history.

I watched the Soviet purges of a generation ago as a worker in Soviet industry, and later as a correspondent.

Unable to get a visa for Mainland China, my observations of recent developments there have been limited to Hong Kong, other peripheral areas, and New York.

Talking with the scholar-experts in Hong Kong, Tokyo, Taipei and Bangkok, interviewing recent arrivals from Mainland China, and reading the voluminous transcripts of Chinese radio broadcasts aimed at their own people, and the dogged, drum-beat editorials from the Chinese press, I was astonished at what took place.

Some examples:

On January 22, 1967, the *Liberation Daily,* organ of China's Communist army, wrote: "We, the People's Liberation Army, must follow Chairman Mao's teachings and enthusiastically, unequivocally and wholeheartedly support the proletarian revolutionary rebels in rising to seize power. Even though they may be just a minority temporarily, we must support them without the slightest hesitation. . . ." Against whom were these "revolutionary rebels" revolting? From what majority group were they trying to seize power? From the Communist Party, in this case in Kwangtung province. And in following out these orders, thousands of Chinese workers and Communist functionaries were killed by soldiers of the Chinese Red Army under the orders of Mao Tse-tung and his heir apparent Lin Piao.

In other provinces, Mao's revolutionary rebels did not succeed in taking power, and army units were not available or were not considered politically reliable enough to support the Maoists against entrenched political leadership enjoying some passive support from the population. In still other provinces—in Chinghai, Kansu and Szechuan —anti-Maoists killed local commanders loyal to Mao and stormed Red Guard-run newspapers and offices. In Sinkiang and Tibet, two of China's most distant and exposed provinces, local military and political leaders are defying Mao with the reported quiet support of the neighboring Russians and Indians.

In this manner, fragmentation began many times in China's past. Was the Great Cultural Revolution to initiate still another period of suffering and civil war less than two decades after the Communists succeeded in unifying Mainland China and giving it relatively honest

22

centralized government for the first time in a century? If so, what an utterly irrational and self-defeating way for the Chinese people, nearly one-quarter of the human race, to try to solve their immense primary problem—feeding themselves on their eroded and battle-scarred land.

Why are there so many Chinese? How have they clung so long and successfully to their ancient culture? In short, how did China become the immense problem that it is for itself and for its neighbors?

Most important to Americans now fighting and dying in a war close to China and actively supported by the Chinese, what is China's future?

In the following pages I shall try to answer these questions.

1. THE LAND IS LARGE, ITS HISTORY LONG

FROM RECENT DIGGINGS, dated with radioactive carbon, we know that some seven thousand years ago men lived on the plains of North China. They had dogs and pigs, wove hemp, made simple implements to help them hunt and fish and protect themselves from predators. These mesolithic savages may have been descended from Sinanthropus Pekinensis—whose 360,000-year-old remains have been found near Peking—though several glacial ages had intervened, and had probably driven man further south.

We know that about five thousand years ago, early Chinese settled along the banks of the Yellow River and began to plant crops, to build simple houses and to pass on from generation to generation legends and sagas about themselves and their world. These stories, written down long afterwards, show some similarities with those of the ancient Chaldeans, Egyptians and others who, many generations earlier, had settled and founded civilizations on the Nile, the Tigris, the Euphrates and, the Indus. The Great Flood is common to most, as is the concept of original chaos. This would suggest that, though separated by the world's highest mountains and broadest deserts, there may have been contact between the ancient Chinese and their cousins in the Eastern Mediterranean and Middle East, or that they may have had certain major, parallel experiences.

Even in its legendary period, however, from about 2850

to 2205 B.C., Chinese folklore makes no mention of any other civilization. The epics and stories that come down from this pre-dynastic period describe how Taimat, the Goddess of Chaos—a huge dragon—was made pregnant by the wind Ch'i, the immortal principle, and gave birth to Yin and Yang—a sort of abstract Chinese Adam and Eve. Yang, the positive, is symbolized by the hills, the sun, strength; Yin, the negative, is symbolized by valleys, rivers, storms, vegetation.

From the union of Yang and Yin came Pan Ku, the ancient architect. It was he who made order out of chaos. With his mallet and chisel he worked for eighteen thousand years, shaping the great blocks of granite that he found floating in space. After thus creating the universe, he died. His head became our mountains; his breath, the winds; his voice, thunder. His left eye became the sun; his right, the moon; his beard became the stars; his veins, the rivers; his sweat, the rain; his flesh, the soil. The lice that infested his body became human beings. In this way does ancient Chinese legend explain the origin of our race.

The Hsia Dynasty began around 2205 B.C. For five hundred years it lasted. Agriculture improved. Black pottery appeared. Then, after a period of war in the eighteenth century B.C., came the Shang Dynasty—and the beginning of Chinese written history. Barter trade was carried on, and bronze vessels were made, as well as ornaments. Carved ivory and jade appeared, as did the first picture writing, which came more than a thousand years after the first Egyptian hieroglyphics and early Chaldean and Summerian clay tablets.

The dates of the Shang Dynasty are traditionally fixed as 1766 to 1122 B.C., but some modern scholars set the dates as 1523 to 1027 B.C. During these years, a series of kings exercised varying degrees of authority over the growing community, which spread southward to the Yangtze valley. Gradually the Shang kings became corrupt, and probably their power was eroded by the floods and the famines that even then plagued China's river valleys. After a period of rebellion and strife, a new dynasty, the Chou, came to power. By this time the pattern for China's history had become fairly well established—

hereditary monarchy, punctuated by periods of instability, peasant uprisings, fragmentation of the country into warring provinces, then consolidation by a new dynasty of rulers.

The Chou Dynasty was one of China's most productive. During its early years, cities grew up on both the Yellow and Yangtze rivers. Iron was smelted and forged into tools and weapons. Scholars, poets and writers appeared. China's first book, *The Book of Changes* (I Ching), was written in 1150 B.C. But this was many centuries after the first collections of ancient wisdom—for example, the stories and philosophy of the Old Testament—had been formulated and written in the Mediterranean Basin.

Under the early Chou Dynasty, great feudal states grew up, and under the late Chou, they quarreled and fought among themselves. It was during this unhappy period of war—pestilence added to the troubles—that several great leaders and philosophers appeared, formulating systems of belief and behavior that exercise profound influence over the Chinese to this day. As the Greek philosopher Heraclitus would note later, "Minerva's owls take flight in gathering darkness"—thinkers appear in troubled times. Perhaps it was the disorder and strife of the late Chou Dynasty that prodded these early Chinese wise men to grope for patterns of behavior to assure harmony and order for man.

The first was Lao Tzu. Born in 604 B.C. in the state of Ch'u (in today's Central China), he taught that man can live in harmony only if he obeys the Way of Tao. By practicing "action by inaction," peace in adversity can be achieved. Lao Tzu was the first to formulate the Golden Rule and to urge all to "repay hatred with kindness." As a librarian and historian for one of the Chou kings, he studied the wisdom of the past, contemplated the basic unity of life, and dreamed of the perfection to come. Toward the end of his life he wrote the *Tao Te Ching* or "Book of Taoist Virtue," a great mystical work. Lao Tzu himself stated that it defied study, and like most such teachings, it contained contradictions and unclarities. But its admonitions of charity, benevolence, virtue and responsibility had much in common with the teachings of

27

Jesus Christ some five hundred years later, although Lao Tzu did not recognize a god.

The second great teacher to emerge during this period was Kung Fu-tzu, or Confucius, who was born in what is now Shantung province, about 551 B.C. Very little is positively known about his life. According to lore, Confucius was born into a poor but respected family. He decided to become a scholar at the age of fifteen, and by twenty-one, students were already seeking his wisdom. Tradition also says that he became a minister of state and that his well-governed district became the wonder of the land. It is said that intrigue and slander forced him to resign, and it was then that he began to wander, teaching the five virtues: kindness, uprightness, decorum, wisdom and truth—the Way of Heaven. Historians base what they know about Confucius on the *Analects,* a collection of sayings and short dialogues collected by his pupils. What is known is that Confucius rejected metaphysics and spirits. He opposed revolutionary acts. He taught reverence for parents, living or dead, but he did not believe in immortality. A sensible middle-of-the-roader, Confucius became the philosopher of the status quo. He died when he was around seventy, practically unknown.

The teachings of Lao Tzu and Confucius were similar. Both contributed a great deal by giving the Chinese people the humility to endure what for millions of them was an exceptionally hard life, and the wisdom to help each other under the most adverse conditions. Both men were pragmatists and humanists. Yet around their teachings, no saints or priests emerged to use them as a ladder to power and wealth.

This was not the case with the teachings of another great philosopher who was a contemporary of Confucius but not a native of the same country—the Buddha, or Gautama, of India. Buddha was born as Prince Siddhartha in what is now Nepal in the sixth century B.C. His family belonged to the second highest caste in Indian society. The traditional story is that while still a young man, Buddha rejected the wealth and power of his parents. He spent six quiet years in reflection, living like a hermit in the forest, before his famous discovery under the *bodhi,* or sacred fruit tree, of the Truth. Then he went forth to teach the people of India his beliefs. He left no works in his own hand. His disciples attribute to him many startling observations on a wide variety of subjects. For one, "Matter is made up of an infinite number of atoms in constant motion through the larger space which separates them. . . ." He taught restraint, friendliness, compassion and knowledge. He taught that men are reborn after death in a series of reincarnations. In each reincarnation men are rewarded for virtue by being advanced toward nirvana or they are punished for misconduct by demotion to a lower form of life.

Buddhism did not come to China until the first century A.D. But by then, in Nepal and Tibet and later in India, Burma, Ceylon, Thailand and Cambodia, Buddhist temples had already sprung up with golden images, with elaborate ritual and with a numerous church hierarchy. This hierarchy could be quarrelsome and stoutly asserted its monopoly over the interpretation of the Buddha's teaching.

Though Buddhism never became as popular in China as Taoism or Confucianism, many Chinese adopted its teachings toward the end of their lives. Contemporary critics have remarked that when in power, the Chinese tend to embrace Confucianism, because it supports the status quo; when out of power, they lean toward Taoism because of its acceptance of the Way; when old, they become Buddhists because of the promise of reincarnation and eventual nirvana.

The Chou Dynasty produced a rich array of early poets. Much of their work reflected a respect for contemplation, a mature appreciation of man's problems in mastering his own imperfections, of knowing himself. Yang Tsu, for example, in the fourth century B.C., wrote a poem entitled "On Being Sixty," which goes, in part: (as translated by Arthur Waley)

> Between thirty and forty one is distracted by the five lusts;
> Between seventy and eighty one is prey to a hundred diseases.
> But from fifty to sixty one is free from all ills,
> Calm and still, the heart enjoys rest.

I have put behind me love and greed.
I have done with profit and fame . . .

Other poets, in a role that has been the mark of great writers throughout history, began to criticize the establishment and its accepted doctrines. At that time, the accepted philosophy was the do-goodism of Confucius and Lao Tzu. Poet-philosopher Chuang Tzu, in the third century B.C., expressed a sophisticated cynicism in his poem "Born in Sin." This was to be echoed centuries later in the concept of original sin in Christendom.

By nature, man is evil. If man is good,
    that is an accident.
His is influenced first of all,
    by a desire for gain.
Hence he strives to get all he can
    without consideration for his neighbor.
Secondly, he is liable to envy and hate; he seeks the
        ruin of others, and loyalty and truth are set aside.
Thirdly, he is a slave to his animal passions; hence he
    commits excesses, and wanders from the path of duty
    and right.
Thus conformity with man's natural disposition leads to
    all kinds of violence, disorder and ultimate barbarism.

The Chou Dynasty fell in 403 B.C. For almost two hundred years, China suffered through the so-called Warring States period, followed by two extraordinary dynasties, beginning in 221 B.C. with the short-lived Ch'in. One of the Ch'in rulers took the title of Shih Huang Ti, which means "the First Emperor." He was determined that his reign would go down in history as the beginning of the Chinese Empire. The name China is taken from Ch'in, the title of his dynasty. He was actually the fourth ruler of that dynasty. To break all connections with the past, he ordered the destruction of historical books. Only some of the classics were burned, but the Emperor's intent was clear. He broke up the feudal states by force and did accomplish the unification of China. It was Shih Huang Ti who began the Great Wall of China to protect the country from the rapacious raiders who had been sweeping down from the plains of what are now Mongolia and

Siberia to pillage the increasingly prosperous farming communities and cities in the river valleys and along the coast.

Shih Huang Ti's tyrannical rule roused massive unrest, which led three years after his death to bloody conflict and to the founding of a new dynasty in 202 B.C.—the Han Dynasty. The Han's attempted the unification of China, not by force and violence, but by scholarship and by editing of the kind to which the Chinese seem particularly suited. Literary and historical documents that survived the "First Emperor" were rewritten to fit the new dynasty's ideas of Chinese history. During this time Confucianism was declared the official religion of the country. One can understand now why so much of early Chinese history is questioned by modern scholars and why so many historical accounts of China are prefaced by the expression, "According to tradition . . ."

It was during this time that the meritorious system of philosopher-civil servant, appointed after highly competitive examinations, became established as the arm of government in China.

The Han Dynasty, which lasted four centuries, pushed the frontiers of China far to the west, into what is now Soviet Kazakhstan, then northward into Korea, and southward into Vietnam. Science was encouraged and flourished; the compass and paper were invented; money, weights and measures were standardized. The Chinese ideographs were stylized and standardized so that literate men could communicate over the vast empire—as extensive as was its contemporary, the Roman Empire in the Mediterranean—even though the languages the Chinese spoke were often as different as Latin and Aramaic.

The Han Dynasty was divided into two periods: the Earlier and the Later. The Earlier Han's terminated in A.D. 9, with the seizure of the throne by a nephew of the Han Empress. Radical reforms were introduced, including a movement to distribute land to the peasants. This was one of the first agrarian revolutions. When it ended with the nephew's assassination in A.D. 25, the Han Dynasty was restored as the Later Dynasty. In a vigorous expansion of power, it extracted tribute from Afghanistan; its merchant ships penetrated into the Indian Ocean.

Gradually the treasury was depleted by conquest and

the defense of the country from the Hsiung-nu, or Huns, who periodically came surging down over the Great Wall. As the population in the river valleys grew, it became more vulnerable to famine after floods. The rivers had to be contained in expensive dikes as the silt raised the level of the water and floods became more frequent. These disasters led to revolts, and finally, in A.D. 220, to the collapse of one of China's most productive dynasties.

There followed four centuries of chaos, sometimes known as the Period of the Three Kingdoms and the Six Dynasties. Dynasties coexisted and warred, and barbarian invasions forced mass migrations from the Yellow River Valley all the way down to the Yangtze. Not until A.D. 619 did the Empress Wu consolidate power over China and found the T'ang Dynasty.

China had now reached the noontide of its civilization, while Europe was at its early dawn. The beginning of the seventh century heralded an era of glorious cultural achievement in China, the greatest of all being literature, particularly poetry. It was said of this age, "Whoever was a man, was a poet." Indeed, China boasted a colossal army of poets. *The Anthology of the T'ang Dynasty* consists of nine hundred books, containing more than 48,900 poems by no less than 2,300 poets! Of this extraordinary number, the two most distinguished were Li Po and Tu Fu. Li Po is generally regarded as the greatest Chinese poet of all time. Friends and contemporaries, these two dreamer-poets tippled their way through pleasant, contemplative lives.

A sample by Tu Fu:

THE VIEW OF THE WILDERNESS
Snow is white on the westward mountains and on
   three fortified towns.
And waters in this southern lake flash on a long
   bridge.
But wind and dust from sea to sea bar me from
   brothers;
And I cannot help crying, I am so far away.
I have nothing to expect now but the ills of old age.
I am of less use to my country than a grain of dust.
I ride out to the edge of town. I watch on the horizon,
Day after day, the chaos of the world.

Li Po was similarly inclined. One of his most famous poems follows:

DRINKING ALONE WITH THE MOON

From a pot of wine among the flowers
I drank alone. There was no one with me—
Till, raising my cup, I asked the bright moon
To bring me my shadow and make us three.
Alas, the moon was unable to drink
And my shadow tagged me vacantly;
But still for a while I had these friends
To cheer me through the end of spring . . .
I sang. The moon encouraged me.
I danced. My shadow tumbled after.
As long as I knew, we were companions.
. . . Shall goodwill ever be secure?
I watch the long road of the River of Stars.

Li Po is supposed to have drowned in a river as he attempted, while drinking, to embrace the reflection of the moon in the water.

Toward the end of the T'ang Dynasty, an event took place that was symbolic of the fact that at this stage in history, the Chinese were the world's most advanced civilization. In 868 the first book was printed, some 500 years before the famed Gutenberg Bible in Europe.

The T'ang Dynasty was overthrown by hungry peasants, scheming courtiers and greedy concubines. Still another period of chaos followed: the Five Dynasties, from 907 to 960. During this period Chinese women began to suffer one of the most cruel rituals in history—foot binding. Far earlier, women had earned men's anger. Confucius is quoted as saying: "Women are very difficult to control. . . . At the bottom of every trouble there is a woman. Suffer them to be your equal, and they become your superior. . . ." According to an ancient proverb, "A stupid son is better than a clever daughter." The drowning of newborn girls in hungry years had been practiced in China since the earliest days. In China's patriarchal society, the oldest male member of each family was its unquestioned dictator, and daughters, and particularly daughters-in-law, were little more than servants. But foot binding not only imposed constant torture on girls from an early age, but condemned them to spend the rest of their lives as hobbling semi-invalids.

In 960 a dynasty was founded that established control over all China and gave the country three centuries of peace and further development. This was the Sung Dynasty. During its time gun powder was used for the first time for military purposes. But it was also a period of artistic progress. Painting and poetry flourished, often wedded, as artists decorated their delicate landscapes and pastoral scenes with exquisitely brushed verses. Paper currency and movable type were invented. A new popular literary form appeared—the novel. One of the earliest was a great classic of Chinese literature entitled *All Men Are Brothers* (also known as *Water Margin*) by Shih Nai-an. It is a long epic novel describing with detailed realism the guerrilla warfare used during the dynastic conflicts of earlier years. It is interesting and symbolic that not only is none of the main characters in the story a foreigner, but the "War and Peace" length book contains not a single mention of people or events non-Chinese.

Most of the accomplishments of the Sung Dynasty occurred during its early, relatively stable period. In 1260 came disaster. For the first time in China's history the country was conquered by a foreign race. Mongol hordes swept into China from the north and west, innundated the Great Wall, and moved into Peking under Ghengis Khan. They rode on tough little horses and carried bows and arrows. They were skillful, dauntless fighters, with an elite officer corps. Barbarian invasions had come before, of course, but had usually been repulsed, or absorbed without seriously interfering with the sweep of China's history. This time the brutal horsemen came well-led, well-disciplined, with an iron will to take over China and all the world. After quickly taking control of the country's complacent and flabby bureaucracy, the Great Khan and his successors of the Yuan Dynasty went out to conquer the known world in a burst of martial energy surpassing even that of the Macedonians under Alexander, or of early Islam. The Mongols overran Russia and pushed into what are now Poland and Rumania. Mobile task forces spearheaded out across the Danube and reached the Adriatic. At that point the Great Khan died, and his frontline commanders rode off across half of Europe and all of Asia, back to the capital. Though the Mongols and their Tartar and other Turkic cousins remained in control of much of Russia and collected tribute from local kings as far into Europe as Germany for two centuries, their control was gradually eroded. They left behind them in Russia a heritage of hostility still important today.

The Yuan emperors did not limit themselves to westward conquests. They went southward, conquered Burma, and raided into Bengal. Marco Polo, on his way back to Europe from the court of the Khan, witnessed in 1272 an epic battle in which Burmese mounted on elephants were defeated by the doughty Mongol archers on their sturdy horses. Another army conquered Korea and tried unsuccessfully to invade Japan. Still another spearhead penetrated through Vietnam, down across the golden peninsula through what is now Thailand and Malaysia and into the Majahapit Empire, which, in those days, controlled most of the Indonesian archipelago. For a century the Majahapit kings paid tribute to Peking.

The accomplishments of Kublai Khan and his successors went beyond military conquest. They built thousands of miles of roads, and vastly improved China's canal system. Chinese merchant ships crossed the Indian Ocean, establishing regular contacts with the Arab states on the Persian Gulf. They improved the civil service system and reversed Chinese tradition by welcoming foreigners to their ports and court.

But the vigor and discipline of the Mongol leaders were gradually eroded by the pleasures of court life. And the people were not enthusiastic about paying the heavy taxes and military conscriptions which the Khan's endless wars demanded.

In 1368, a Buddhist novice of peasant origin—his name was Chu Yuan-chang—organized a rebellion, forced the Mongols from Peking, and founded the Ming Dynasty. The Mongols, like other earlier invaders, were far less numerous than the Chinese, and they lacked the Chinese patience and stoic stamina. In the end, neither their primitive culture nor their violent physical presence left much impression on the Chinese.

Under the Ming emperors, the Chinese Empire extended from Burma to Korea, while its navies and merchantmen raided and traded as far as West Africa. Japan paid tribute to Peking. At the same time the Moguls, cousins of the Chinese—though not politically or administratively associated with the Ming Empire—established control over Afghanistan and most of northern India.

The world's finest pottery and porcelain were produced in the late Ming period. Indeed it was under the Mings that porcelain became known as "china" throughout the world. Highly skilled craftsmen turned out superb sculpture and architecture—exquisite carvings in stone, wood and jade—unmatched lacquers, enamels and tapestries. A small but affluent literate minority had the money to support these creative artists. They also had the taste and discrimination to encourage quality. Chinese society as a whole, based on the productive agriculture of the valleys and plains, could support the wealthy bureaucracy and its cultural entourage without mass hunger—except when the floods came. But China was large, and its economy decentralized. Flood and famine could decimate one province, and the rest of the country might know little of the tragedy.

Ming translated is "bright" in Chinese, and during this dynasty the arts and sciences flourished. China's art has traditionally sought to depict tranquility. Rural and pastoral scenes emphasize the grandeur of mountains, the delicate texture of birds' feathers and of flowers, and the gentle pressures of wind on trees. Confucius had said, "The wise find pleasure in waters, the virtuous in hills. . . ." Under the Mings, while soldiers and sailors on frontiers of the empire pushed vigorously forward, the bulk of Chinese society—and nearly all its art and literature—was turned inward. The painter and philosopher Shen Chou (1427-1509) described his idyllic way of life: "One flower, one bamboo, one lamp and one small table, books of poems. . . . My friends are farmers, my conversation with mountains. News of the world does not enter my gate. Should it intrude, the breeze of the pines would waft it away. . . ." Chinese artists were loathe to depict conflict, for this would violate Confucius' principles of restraint and propriety.

But new forces, both internal and external, began to make themselves felt. The Mings endeavored to exclude foreigners from the land, but a European settlement was made by the Portuguese at Macao in 1557. Missionaries also appeared, and in 1582, one of them, a Jesuit priest named Matteo Ricci, received permission to open the first Christian mission in China. Ricci became a favorite of the Emperor and succeeded in introducing Christianity into Chinese cities. The influence of these early Europeans on China, however, was negligible.

During the Ming Dynasty, three centuries of internal peace made possible a rapid increase in population. Peasants farmed limited areas along the coast and the big river systems, and they exerted pressures leading to gradual impoverishment as millions were squeezed into smaller and smaller farms. Often forced to sell their daughters into concubinage, and ground down by their wealthier neighbors, the debt-ridden peasant millions began to form that stubborn, sullen and resilient mass out of which Mao Tse-tung was to build his revolutionary armies.

The Mings had begun their dynasty by successfully driving out a foreign conqueror. They ended when a second foreign conqueror drove them out. The later years of the Mings were marred by corruption in the court and by peasant revolts in the countryside. These were conditions the Manchus from Manchuria exploited to advantage. The Manchus captured Peking in 1644. Within fifteen years they had occupied all of China. The rule they established is known as the Ch'ing Dynasty. Under this dynasty, China reached its zenith in territorial control. At the end of it, China was to experience the most humiliating and disastrous defeat of its history.

During the time of the Manchu conquest, a precedent-establishing episode occurred—at the time a passing detail in a series of mopping up operations that involved disorders in the south of China and, in particular, a certain offshore island.

A Ming general named Cheng Ch'eng-kung—alias Koxinga—had been defeated by the Manchus and had escaped with his army to the island of Taiwan (Formosa), where he had established himself. He tried to organize a Ming restoration and launched an invasion of the mainland, but was beaten back. After Koxinga's death in 1662, dissension broke out among his successors. In 1683, a Manchu force invaded the island and occupied this last Ming stronghold. Taiwan was incorporated into the Manchu Empire and remained under its jurisdiction until 1895.

Without being as oppressive or cruel as the Mongols, the Manchus did pursue foreign conquest. They established control over much of what is now Soviet Central Asia and over a great deal of Eastern Siberia. They conquered Tibet and parts of northern Burma.

The early years of the Manchu Dynasty were creative. Porcelain production in both quality and quantity reached a glorious high point. The first fairly complete dictionary was published in China in 1716. It listed 47,000 characters, with an explanation of the meaning of each. The Chinese dictionary preceded Samuel Johnson's by several decades. (The average dictionary in use today in China has only some 10,000 characters, while daily newspapers use about 5,000.)

The peasant masses, on the other hand, were illiterate and superstitious. For them there was no respite in the eternal battle against flood and famine. As they grew ever more numerous, hunger haunted them constantly, so much so that even today when a Chinese meets another, his greeting often is *Ni-chih-kuo-le-ma?*—"Have you eaten?"

Though China is large—roughly 4 per cent larger than the United States—most of the land is either too high or too arid for cultivation. Only 11 per cent of its area is considered arable, only 10 per cent is forested. These are facts of geography that make the country more than usually vulnerable to flooding.

Egypt and Mesopotamia are largely deserts and also endure periodic floods. But the early civilizations in these areas did not survive military defeat, internal disorder, famine and pestilence which destroyed the fabric of their civilization and so reduced their populations as to diminish the pressure for food. Modern Iraq, for example, has some 7 million people. In the tenth century, before the great Mongol invasions, the population was probably 30 million, living with the help of an elaborate irrigation system begun in antiquity. The Mongol invaders of the

38

thirteenth century destroyed the canals; three-quarters of the population died or fled.

It is the very resilience of the Chinese, their stubborn immunity to many infections that have killed others, and the durability of their culture, built around Confucian patience and filial responsibility, protected by the isolation of centuries, which caused them to face, in about the middle of the Manchu Dynasty, the realities of Malthus' theory about the relationship of people to land. There were more Chinese than could be adequately fed on their land at their level of technology. And there was nowhere else to go. Toward the middle of the nineteenth century, China's per capita production of food began to decline. It has been falling ever since.

During the middle of the Manchu Dynasty, however, China's rulers and the establishment were preoccupied with the pleasant life and self-admiration, complacently certain that China—Chung Kuo—the Middle Kingdom, embodied the only worthwhile cultural and scientific achievements in the world. Looking back, as they could, on long centuries of achievement, the Chinese regarded all others as barbarians. To pay attention to other cultures in Europe and in the Western Hemisphere—of which the Chinese were vaguely conscious—was a waste of time. To study them and their activities was unthinkable.

This blinding self-admiration was based on a fatal misapprehension. About the time the Manchus had come to power in China, a burst of scientific and cultural energy had begun in Europe. It was to alter completely man's relations with nature, and his capacity to modify his environment. But the Chinese, smugly certain that they already knew everything worth knowing, had stopped making new inventions; they had ceased prodding into the frontiers of knowledge or of their world.

The rude awakening came in the nineteenth century, and its full effects have still to be measured.

2. A CENTURY OF SHAME AND HUMILIATION

EUROPEAN MARITIME POWERS were attracted by China's luxury goods, particularly its porcelain, silk and tea. But the Manchu Emperors were opposed to trade with any foreign power. However, in 1751, an imperial edict permitted maritime trade in a special area along the Pearl River in Canton. Here, foreign merchants were allowed to buy the luxury goods they wanted. But they were permitted to deal only with a trade monopoly organization authorized by the Emperor, and were forced to pay for their purchases in silver. Imports were forbidden. The "barbarians" were not allowed to travel within China, and it was illegal for any Chinese to teach a foreigner the Chinese language.

At the time, the Europeans were penetrating into other parts of the world in highly aggressive competition for markets and spheres of influence. Britain's King George III took the initiative in seeking to open the doors of China by sending Lord Macartney, an able and trusted emissary, to Peking in 1793. Macartney brought gifts for the Emperor and proposals of increased trade.

The British emissary was granted one imperial audience, along with other "barbarian" representatives from Mongolia and Burma. During this interview the Emperor acknowledged the British sovereign's "humility and obedience" in paying tribute to himself, but he emphasized that neither increase in trade relations nor relaxation in the restrictions on foreign traders could be expected, since the

Emperor saw no need to import any of Britain's m
factures. Before his departure, Macartney was told that if
King George should find the wisdom to swear perpetual
obedience to the Emperor, Britain would undoubtedly
prosper.

A later mission, undertaken in 1816 by Lord Amherst,
was no more successful in penetrating China's stubborn
isolation. But by that time, a highly significant transforma-
tion was taking place in China's trade patterns: the introduction of opium as an import with which to pay for the
tea and silk and ceramics so much in demand in Europe.
This opium trade was illicit from the beginning, as Imperial edict restricted the drug to medical use in China.
But addiction grew rapidly among China's hungry,
crowded, urban masses, and corrupt officials, eager for
bribes, cooperated so effectively that by the 1830s, more
than 3 million pounds of raw opium were being imported
annually. It was not only enough to pay for China's exports, but silver began to flow out of China, to the profit
of the eager European merchants.

Aroused, the Emperor appointed an outstanding official
to Canton with orders to confiscate all opium and to
behead anyone caught trafficking in it. Foreign merchants
watched powerlessly as $11 million worth of the stuff
was seized and publicly destroyed. Then they withdrew to
the nearby islands of Macao and Hong Kong and continued their profitable trade in defiance of the Chinese
authorities and under the protection of their own military
power.

The Opium War followed. It lasted from 1839 until
1842 and ushered in a century of shameful Western aggression against China and humiliating defeats suffered by
that huge country, whose moribund Manchu rulers seemed
incapable of defending themselves.

For three years the British moved warships into the
harbors of Amoy and Shanghai, occupying positions at
will. They sailed up the Yangtze to the sometime capital
of Nanking without meeting any effective resistance from
the Emperor's troops.

When Nanking fell under the enemy guns, the Emperor moved to buy off the invaders, as his predecessors
had sometimes done with other barbarian invaders. But

this time the price was high. The Emperor ceded to Britain the island of Hong Kong in perpetuity, and opened five major Chinese ports for trade and foreign residence. Not only could foreigners live legally in these cities, but their persons and their businesses fell under the jurisdiction of their own courts to whom the Chinese authorities surrendered effective power. The Emperor agreed to pay the British an indemnity of $21 million, while nothing at all was said about the opium trade, which continued profitably.

Shocked and humiliated, the Emperor tried to organize his administration and his people. Bled for decades by periodic floods and famines, by high rents, interest and oppressive taxation, the peasantry was in no mood to respond, while the corrupt and tradition-bound officials were as incapable of coping with the new ideas rapidly seeping into China as they were with British gunboats. Bands of anti-Manchu brigands burned and looted their way through many provinces.

Then, beginning in 1850, China suffered one of the most bloody and irrational disasters in its history, the T'ai P'ing Rebellion. A Cantonese schoolmaster named Hung Hsiu-ch'uan—who had fallen under the influence of an American missionary and of Western books—had visions, during an illness, which convinced him that he was in fact the younger brother of Jesus Christ, whose mission it was to bring T'ai P'ing, or "Heavenly Peace," to China. With a band of converts to whom he preached a confused and inflammatory mixture of Christian and Taoist doctrine, Hung swept northward, gathering followers as he went, many because of his agrarian reforms. He took Nanking in 1853 and held it as his capital for the next eleven years, while his armies burned and looted their way through much of China.

Once again, a Chinese dynasty demonstrated resilience and stubborn survival power. The Emperor and his administration—with the aid of the famous British general, Charles Gordon, and the American military adventurer, Frederick Ward—successfully regrouped their forces in 1864 and laid siege to Nanking. Hung Hsiu-ch'uan poisoned himself during the battle, and his few remaining followers were driven into the mountains.

The rebellion cost China an estimated 20 million lives. It solved nothing. More serious, the Europeans continued pressing still more demands. During the 1850s and '60s, the foreigners—now joined by the Russians—sent thirty gunboats and several thousand troops, forcing the Emperor to open eleven more ports and to agree to permit both traders and missionaries to operate all over China. When the Emperor balked at allowing foreign ambassadors to reside in Peking, foreign troops marched into the city and destroyed the Imperial Summer Palace. The Emperor was even forced to surrender control of his own customs service to foreign officials.

A few years later the Japanese joined the action. They pushed into Korea, and when the Chinese resisted, crushed the Emperor's armies. In 1894 they forced him to cede to them Taiwan, the Pescadores and parts of Manchuria, as well as effective control of all of Korea.

A number of idealistic and patriotic Chinese intellectuals realized that China must adjust to Western ways or suffer even greater losses. In 1898 these reformers succeeded in capturing the imagination of young Emperor Kuang Hsu who inaugurated a sweeping program of modernization, involving industry, agriculture and education as well as administration. But entrenched officials, whose positions and privileges would have been endangered, used the old Empress Dowager to stage a counterattack, and after only one hundred days Kuang Hsu was in prison and his reforms repudiated.

Meanwhile, the foreigners' appetites were insatiable. The Russians wanted a railroad in Manchuria; the French, exclusive development rights in South China; the Germans, mines in Shantung; the British, new territories adjacent to Hong Kong and concessions in the Yangtze valley. Only the United States, in part at least because of preoccupation at the time with the development of its own country, refrained from making demands on the helpless Chinese, and urged the prohibition of all exclusive concessions under an "Open Door Policy."

Millions of Chinese were understandably incensed at the foreigners for thus carving up and devouring China's living body. Poorly articulated secret societies began to agitate for revenge, not only against the foreigners, but against

Chinese who had been converted to Christianity. One of the most important of these was a group of fanatics who became known as the "Boxers" because they engaged in ceremonial shadow-boxing which, they believed, made them invulnerable to bullets. In 1899, advisers persuaded the senile Empress to give the Boxers her official support, and thus encouraged, they organized a rebellion which captured Peking in June, 1900, and laid siege to the foreign quarter until an eight-nation expeditionary force arrived and scattered them. Few foreigners were killed in this rebellion but the Chinese converts were not so fortunate; thousands perished. In the wake of this senseless and destructive violence, China was forced to agree to pay $739 million in indemnities, and a section of central Peking was designated for foreigners. Henceforth, no Chinese were to live in this district. The United States allocated its share of the indemnity for scholarships to Chinese youths.

The numbers of Chinese revolutionists were growing, and some were forming organizations. Among the most effective individuals was a young physician, Dr. Sun Yat-sen, a Christian convert whose studies in China and in London had included extensive reading of such authors as Karl Marx and Henry George. During the first decade of the century, Sun and his followers sparked a number of minor revolts in many parts of China, and Sun himself traveled to overseas Chinese communities around the world, raising money for his cause and trying to persuade foreign governments that the interests of all concerned could be best served by the overthrow of the moribund Manchu Dynasty and the formation of a republic.

In 1911, an uprising in Wuchang turned into a full-scale revolution, and on December 24, 1911, the Manchu Dynasty at last fell. Sun Yat-sen became First President of the Republic of China.

But Sun had no administrative experience, no mass political backing, and most important, no army. Furthermore, during the slow disintegration of the Manchu authority, a number of reasonably strong provincial governors and military leaders, or War Lords, had entrenched themselves. These were disinclined to subordinate themselves to a young Christian-doctor-idealist. Although Sun reorganized his secret revolutionary society into a political party, the Kuomintang, or "National People's Party" (KMT), he was unable to unify China or prevent continued local wars. Then, he himself was forced from the presidency and obliged to flee the country in 1912. He spent most of the following decade in and out of exile, trying to organize an effective party and a government dedicated to his three "Principles": nationalism, democracy, and improved welfare for the people through land reforms and controls over the economy. War Lords fought each other throughout the decade; foreign businessmen exploited and enlarged their concessions; while at the same time foreign missionaries and educators established some excellent schools, a number of modern hospitals and other institutions. In big coastal cities like Shanghai, textile and other industries appeared, organized and run by foreigners or by enterprising Chinese, while in the North, in Manchuria, the foundation was laid for a coal-based heavy industry.

In 1922, a young officer named Chiang Kai-shek, a graduate of a Japanese military academy, and a veteran of many revolutionary battles, became closely associated with Sun, and gradually assumed leadership of the Socialist-oriented KMT. The two men married sisters, May-ling and Ching-ling Soong. They were the American-educated, Christian daughters of a famous Chinese business family, and the sisters of T.V. Soong, later China's Minister for Foreign Affairs.

Sun succeeded in 1922 in getting promises of substantial outside military and financial assistance. Since the Western countries saw little advantage in a unified China, it is not surprising that it was Russia, war-torn and isolated, reborn with a new ideology as the Soviet Union, that extended this aid. Due mainly to this Russian support, Chiang Kai-shek, as leader of the KMT, succeeded in wearing down the power of the War Lords and achieved a moderate measure of national unity during the early and mid-1920s.

Sun Yat-sen died of cancer in 1925. His wife survived him. She would emerge—after decades of political cliff-hanging—as the matriarch of Communist China in the 1960s.

Chiang Kai-shek was still working at political consolidation when, in 1937, China was invaded by Japan. For a decade the Japanese killed and looted, forcing millions of Chinese workers to build an impressive industrial empire in Manchuria, geared to supply and supplement Japan's own economy in that Nipponese nirvana—the Greater East Asia Co-Prosperity Sphere. Fighting not only the Chinese, but other enemies as well, the Japanese outdid the nineteenth century Europeans in inflicting indignity and suffering on the Chinese people. During the war, that part of China not occupied by the Japanese was torn by civil war, while its resources, its land and people, became pawns of its Japanese and occidental enemies.

The Chinese were beaten and squeezed, insulted, humiliated, demeaned, mortified, degraded. The Chinese did not have even the dubious satisfaction of being forced to suffer because someone wanted to use their talents, their resources and markets. China had reached that nadir of disintegration where its land and culture had been so destroyed as to be all but worthless to anyone. Chinese were worth killing only as a by-product of conflicts involving other peoples.

It is a striking tribute to the toughness of the Chinese people, and to the resilience of their national culture, that they were able to survive this horrendous century, and even to increase in numbers during it—from roughly 300 million to more than 500 million. It is a tribute to their patience and character that they retained their sense of humor, their ability to smile tolerantly over the ashes of their homes and the graves of their honored ancestors. The Romans suffered far less at the hands of the Visigoths, and their civilization did not recover.

3. THE COMMUNISTS WIN

MAO TSE-TUNG was born in 1893 in Hunan, the eldest son of a poor peasant family. Mao learned to hate his barely literate but ambitious and tyrannical father, who beat his sons for laxity in their studies or in helping farm the family's three acres. Mao adored his illiterate Buddhist mother and embraced her faith until he left home in 1912 for Normal School in Changsha, forty miles away.

For six years he studied hard, mastering the classics, and taking part in some student revolutionary activities against a local War Lord. He went to Peking in 1919 and took a job as clerk in the university library, which gave him the opportunity to audit courses and to read voraciously. He lived simply and became active in a Marxist study group, one of several that were to form the nucleus of the Communist Party of China (CPC).

Many young Chinese students and intellectuals were groping at that time for a system of beliefs around which to formulate their desires for a new, more modern and more efficient China. Many were incensed at the betrayal of Versailles, which awarded Germany's concessions in China to Japan, and some of them had studied Marx and Lenin. The organizers of the CPC were two agents of the Comintern, sent from Moscow—Grigory Voitinsky and a Dutchman named Sneevliet who went by the name of Maring. In July of 1921, at a meeting in a girls' school in the French concession in Shanghai, these two organizers assembled representatives of Marxist groups which had formed in six cities. The meeting became the First Congress of the CPC. The participants were nearly all intellectuals of peasant origin, rather than workers. The resolutions passed, however, spoke in Comintern clichés of the historic role of the working class, and provided that the new fledgling party send monthly reports on its activities to headquarters in Moscow. Also implicit from the beginning was the obedience of the Chinese comrades to the senior Comintern representatives in constant residence in China. The most important of these, Mikhail Borodin, soon arrived with instructions to collaborate with the Kuomintang.

These orders irritated Mao and other Chinese Communists who sought to base the Chinese revolution on the peasants. As Mao wrote later: "The peasants are like the raging winds and driving rains . . . no force can stand in their way. . . . Shall we stand in the foreground and lead them, or stand in the background and find ourselves opposing them?"

Mao was uneasy with the city-based KMT. He was suspicious that, in the long run, the Communists would be betrayed. From the beginning, Mao aspired to create and lead an independent and disciplined Communist party. "If we work hard, in thirty or forty years we will be able to rule China," he told a friend in 1921.

Soviet leaders had other ambitions. In 1923, as we have seen, they pledged major aid to the KMT in its drive to unify China. Stalin at that time hoped to use the KMT as Lenin had used the Kerensky government—as a stepping stone to Communist power. Chiang Kai-shek was made commandant of the Whampao Military Academy set up in Canton with a Soviet grant of 3 million rubles and staffed with forty Soviet officers. After 1923, Chinese Communists were ordered to join the KMT as individuals, and to obey its orders and discipline, while maintaining their own secret Communist "fractions." Canton was the seat of the KMT government of South China from 1924 to 1926, while North China was largely controlled by War Lords.

Mao obeyed reluctantly. So did Chou En-lai, a young Chinese intellectual who had joined the Communist Party in France. So did a tough professional soldier named Chu

Teh, who had become a Communist in Germany. So did Liu Shao-chi. From 1923 through 1927, these and other Communists helped the KMT consolidate its position in city after city, and spread its organization into the countryside. Mao himself edited a KMT magazine, and made numerous trips to Canton, Shanghai and Changsha, coordinating the work of the KMT as it struggled against various War Lords to unify China.

Mao's continued contacts with the peasants convinced him that the rural masses were ready to revolt against the landlords and money-lenders who somehow seemed to enjoy the support of the KMT. But in Moscow, Stalin wanted to avoid jeopardizing his cooperation with the KMT, and Mao and other Communists were ordered by Borodin to "restrain" the peasant movement. As in other cases before and afterward, Mao avoided directly disobeying Moscow's orders, while keeping alive the ties and cadres to recreate a newly independent Communist party, should the need arise.

The need came very soon. If the Communists in the KMT had maintained their own secret fractions, Chiang Kai-shek knew it. Besides, he had his own plans and ambitions which he recognized would not be served by a continued Communist presence in his organization.

On April 12, 1927, Chiang moved in Shanghai and other cities in a massive purge of Communists. Thousands were rounded up and summarily executed. Others were tortured to ferret out the names of more comrades. There had been some fifty thousand Communists in early 1927. By summer, only ten thousand were left, and most of them were scattered and out of touch with each other.

Among the survivors was Mao Tse-tung, who fled to the mountains on the borders between Hunan and Kiangsi provinces and set up a headquarters in the village of Chingkangchan. Here he organized about a thousand followers and the nucleus of a guerrilla army. Later in the year he was joined by two groups headed by local peasant-bandits. In 1928, Chu Teh arrived with about two thousand followers. In effect, Mao formed with them the first Communist government in China and set about organizing the military means to defend it against the attacks that were sure to come.

But other Chinese Communist leaders, both those in hiding in the cities, and those who fled the debacle to Moscow, disapproved of Mao's "peasant mentality," and criticized the lack of proletarian leadership in his Kiangsi movement. Mao was expelled from the Party's Politburo, but he did not even hear of the decision for months. He was busy clarifying his thoughts and working out his own revolutionary strategy.

Mao reasoned that the essential purpose of the Party was to seize power. Lenin had made compromises with the peasantry in 1917 by embracing the anti-Marxist slogan "Land to the Peasants." Why should not the Chinese Communists use similar tactics, particularly since the cities had fallen into the hands of the KMT largely due to Moscow's mistakes?

Isolated in his mountain stronghold, Mao sought guidance in the ancient classics for his policies and tactics. Sun Tsu, an important fifth century B.C. Chinese student of military practices, had written, "All warfare is based on deception. Hence when able to attack, we must seem unable; when using our forces, we must seem inactive; when near, we must seem far; when far away, we must make the enemy believe we are near. . . . Feign disorder, and crush the enemy. If he is superior in strength, evade him. If he is of choleric temper, irritate him; pretend to be weak, that he may grow arrogant. If he is inactive, give him no rest."

Mao formulated these classic Chinese admonitions in simpler words:

> The enemy advances: we retreat.
> The enemy halts: we harrass.
> The enemy tires: we attack.
> The enemy retreats: we pursue.

Mao recognized that for at least a time he would be far weaker than his enemies of the KMT, and weaker also than his Moscow-supported opponents in the leadership of the CPC. He knew he must base himself solidly within his environment—in the peasantry. A guerrilla must be at one with the masses, "like a fish in the ocean," he taught. To get along with the peasant masses—treat them fairly; pay for anything you take; support their desires for land reform.

The first of Chiang Kai-shek's "bandit extermination drives" came in 1930. Mao survived the attack by a force many times stronger than his. Then, Moscow-inspired party leadership ordered Mao to counter-attack and capture the cities of Wuhan and Changsha. Realizing that defiance would have meant expulsion, Mao did not protest these orders. He simply disobeyed them. For many months his contacts with other party leaders in China became so tenuous, and his relations with Moscow so strained that at one point Soviet sources announced his death.

But Mao was very much alive. In fact on November 7, 1931, at Tuichin, in Kiangsi province, he proclaimed the "Chinese Soviet Republic." He developed the military means to defend it. He out-maneuvered and out-fought Chiang Kai-shek's punitive expeditions until, gradually, other Communists, in China and Moscow, reluctantly accepted Mao's Chinese Marxism. It seemed to work. By 1933, the CPC boasted 300,000 members, and Mao's armies numbered almost 100,000.

But in his fifth "extermination campaign" Chiang used 400,000 troops—roughly the size of the American force deployed in mid-1967 in Vietnam. The operation was immense, utilizing artillery, air power and modern automatic weapons, many of them of Soviet manufacture. Some fifty thousand of Mao's troops were killed, and perhaps a million peasants in Hunan and Kiangsi died of starvation as a result of military operations. Illness and disagreements with other leaders shook Mao. He probably lost control of his army in early 1934, as the country's first Communist government, with its army, prepared for the historic Long March. The six-thousand-mile march led to Yenan in the mountains of the northwest. Nearly fifty thousand strong, the force set off under the command of Chu Teh, with Chou En-lai as commissar. Breaking out of the Nationalist encirclement, they marched westward for months, harassed by Nationalist attacks, short of food and medical supplies.

In January, 1935, Mao, his health now restored, won control of the Central Committee and remained unquestioned leader of the CPC for more than three decades. After the spectacular crossing of the Tatu River at Luting, the armies turned northward. Losses were frightening, including some close to Mao himself. His younger brother was killed.* Less than seven thousand reached Yenan in late 1935, and set up their government in these distant mountains. But from this group of experienced warriors came the leadership of the CPC and its People's Liberation Army for the next quarter century. It is perhaps because of the heroic magnitude of this common experience that the leadership of the Chinese Communist Party was the most unified in the Communist world and avoided so long the bloody purges that sapped the strength of every other Communist party.

The Chinese Communists had about a year in Yenan to rest and rehabilitate their forces and to gear themselves for more Nationalist attacks. During this year of relative tranquility, Mao acquired a new wife. After bearing him two children and accompanying him on the Long March, Mao's third wife fell ill and was sent to the Soviet Union for medical care. During her absence, a Shanghai film starlet named Lan P'ing came to Yenan. In the austere atmosphere of wartime, an affinity grew. Mao divorced his wife and married the newcomer, who lived with him in loyal anonymity as Chiang Ching until she moved into unexpected prominence during the Great Cultural Revolution thirty years later.

In December, 1936, Chiang Kai-shek was preparing what might have been a decisive campaign against the weakened Communists in Yenan, when a spectacular incident radically changed his plans. He was kidnapped in Sian by one of his own generals and forced to agree to make common cause with the Communists against the Japanese, who were completing their conquest of Manchuria and preparing to invade China itself. In July of 1937 the Japanese did move south on a broad front, taking most of the large cities, seeking to destroy Chiang Kai-shek's armies first because they were nearer than were

---

* Mao's sister was executed by the KMT in 1930, as was his second wife. His second brother was executed in 1942. His third wife—one of thirty-four women to start the long march—survived it. His son was killed in action in Korea in 1950.

the Communists. The Sian incident and the Japanese invasion may well have saved the Communists from destruction.

Disturbed at Japanese aggression so close to their frontiers, the Russians responded by sending nearly $250 million worth of guns, planes and ordnance to China from 1938 until 1941 and insisted that the Chinese Communists enter an anti-Japanese United Front with the KMT. Under this arrangement, Mao's armies were formally merged with the Nationalist armies, though in actual fact they retained their own command structure. For some six years each fought the Japanese in his own way while accusing the other of holding back. The Soviet aid and the American and British assistance, which replaced it after 1941, were channeled almost entirely to Chiang. Very little reached the Communists. Nonetheless, during this United Front period, the CPC was able to consolidate its position and vastly increase its strength in the "liberated" northwest. It was also able to expand its underground organization in other parts of China held by the Japanese and the Nationalists.

By 1940, the People's Liberation Army (PLA) which was what the Communist forces called themselves, numbered 400,000. This was reduced to 300,000 in 1941 by Japan's "3 All" campaign (Burn all. Kill all. Loot all.) Despite these losses, by 1944 the PLA had actually increased to nearly a million. A U.S. Government survey of China made in 1944 and early 1945, which remained "secret" until 1949, characterized China's Communists as "the most effective organized group in China," and the PLA as "the best-led and most vigorous" army in the country, although at the time Chiang Kai-shek's forces were roughly four times as large. The report stated also that the Communists enjoyed more popular support in their territories than did the Nationalists in theirs.

With Japan's defeat in 1945, the situation changed again. Soviet armies invaded Manchuria, disarmed the Japanese, and in some cases turned the weapons over to the PLA. The Russians also took out of Manchuria large quantities of equipment and supplies from the heavy industries there.

At the Seventh Congress of the CPC just after the

Japanese surrender, the "Thoughts of Mao Tse-tung" were officially canonized as the "guide to the entire work of the Party." The cult of Chairman Mao was officially inaugurated by Liu Shao-chi who praised Mao as "not only the greatest revolutionary and statesman, but also the greatest theoretician and scientist of China's history." These claims were still comparatively modest, and did not formally clash with the claims of Stalin, among others, of superlative leadership qualities and achievements on a world scale.

U.S. efforts to persuade the Communists and the Nationalists to cooperate in rebuilding their country were futile. After spending forty-three days in Chung King negotiating with the Nationalists, Mao withdrew and prepared to resume the civil war which had been interrupted by Japan's invasion. Mao now enjoyed a far stronger position than he had in 1937.

Stalin's position was ambivalent. Bled white by the war, Russia was in no position to extend aid to either side. Theoretically, Stalin presumably wanted the Chinese Communists to win. There is some evidence, however, that even then he feared that a victorious Mao would be a potential threat to the U.S.S.R., whereas a victorious Chiang would be merely ineffectual. In any case, Stalin urged Communist cooperation with the Nationalist government, on the grounds that "an uprising in China has no prospect." Once again, Mao simply failed to comply.

In 1946 military operations got under way between a PLA force of about one million and Nationalist forces of about four million. The Nationalists were consistently out-fought. Their conscript armies were poorly disciplined, poorly led, and often faced hostile populations. They were provided with munitions and supplies by the U.S., which spent some $2 billion on various kinds of aid to the Nationalists from World War II's end till 1949. But all too often the supplies were stolen by corrupt officials and officers. Nationalist forces deserted to the enemy in large numbers, and by 1948, in large units. By the end of 1948 the position of the Nationalists had so deteriorated that the numerical ratio between their forces and the PLA stood at about 1:1. Economic disarray swamped what was left of Nationalist China. The "Gold Yuan" issued in April, 1948, and valued at 25¢ U.S., was worth less than 1¢ U.S. a year later. By December of that year the Communists held most of North China, and in January, 1949, the Nationalist garrison in Peking surrendered without firing a shot.

The advancing Communist armies maintained a remarkable discipline. They refrained from the looting and disorder that Chinese armies had traditionally engaged in when taking territory. Communist officials, like Mao himself, were impressively modest and avoided arrogance and ostentatious luxuries.

Chiang now bid for a negotiated settlement, and talks took place for several weeks. But by this time Mao's terms were little short of unconditional surrender, and Chiang rejected them. On April 20th, the PLA crossed the Yangtze on a three-hundred-mile front.

In effect the war was over. Chiang used his remaining resources to flee to Formosa, with his government, its gold reserve and other portable valuables, and nearly a million soldiers and officials and their families. On October 1, 1949, Mao proclaimed the People's Republic of China.

Mao had received little aid from anyone. He had disobeyed Moscow's orders when he thought it best to do so. He had based his revolution on China's peasantry, undisturbed by many critics who accused him of revisionism.

Why was Mao able so decisively to defeat his enemies?

The allegations that he enjoyed more support, better arms, or more money are patently untrue.

Assertions, heard frequently during the Senator McCarthy investigations in the early 1950s, to the effect that subversive miscreants or stupid bunglers in the State Department "betrayed" the Nationalists, are not supported by the evidence. This evidence points rather to the greater skill and dedication of the Communists and the unwillingness or inability of the Nationalists to make reforms in good time.

Communist victory effectively brought all Mainland China under a unified, centralized and disciplined government for the first time in a hundred years.

4. THE COMMUNISTS RULE

A GENERATION OF WAR had destroyed much of China's industry; roads and bridges were in disrepair; railroads barely operated. A large number of the country's technological intelligentsia had fled, and they had taken with them China's gold reserve. Stocks and inventories of all kinds were depleted.

The Communist Party was called in Chinese the *Kungch'antang,* meaning *Kung*—share; *ch'an*—production; *tang*—party, the share production party. By definition it was dedicated to share production, but in late 1949 there was shockingly little production or anything else to share. Power production was down to 72 per cent of the 1942 peak; coal production was 27 million tons—less than half the 1942 figure. Steel production was 162,000 tons, compared to the wartime peak of 900,000 tons. Soviet reparations removals had left China's Manchurian heavy industry base without equipment. Said Mao in early 1950: "It will take about three years to carry out agrarian reform and readjust existing industry and commerce. Conditions for planned economic construction do not yet exist. . . ."

Mao's first step was a visit to Moscow. He did not bow low to the Kremlin, but acknowledged Soviet leadership of the Communist world. After two months of hard bargaining, he obtained a Soviet loan of $300 million for five years, in exchange for Soviet economic concessions in Manchuria. Mao returned to China sobered by this Soviet stinginess to a fledgling brother Communist state.

The next step was land reform. Communist reform teams went from village to village, urging the poor peasants to make public accusations against the local landlords and money lenders and to demand punishment. Mass public trials of the "criminals" followed, the peasants themselves acting as prosecutors, judges and executioners. This form of social surgery followed lines laid down by Mao as early as 1927 when he wrote: "The success of the revolution requires a reign of terror in every rural area to suppress the activities of the counter-revolutionaries and overthrow the authority of the gentry." In the process, millions of peasants emerged with bloody hands. In effect they became Mao's hostages in that they could not now welcome any counter-revolutionary army that might appear, for fear of punishment for their part in the terror.

The Peking government officially admitted 135,000 executions in the first half of 1951 alone. In two years nearly a million people were sent to labor camps. The actual number of victims was certainly much higher. Some scholars put the number killed at 3 million. The results were definitive. By the end of 1951, the landlords and their local supporters had disappeared. Their land—about 100 million acres—was distributed to the peasants. Their other assets—between one and two billion dollars worth —were taken by the state.

In cities and in industry the task before the CPC was more complex. Mao recognized that his still largely peasant party could not take over and run the country's business and industry. Yet even at the expense of some confusion, Mao felt it necessary to take over immediately foreign-owned factories and firms, hospitals, schools and other institutions. Within months these were nationalized and their former owners so belabored with law suits and bills for back pay to disgruntled employees that most employers were lucky to leave the country with nothing but portable personal property.

Chinese businessmen fared far better—in the beginning. They were encouraged to form associations, chambers of commerce and even small political parties and were urged to get their plants back into production. Many who had fled fearfully to Hong Kong returned in this climate of conciliation and went to work as "national businessmen." But their respite ended abruptly in 1952 with the "3 anti" and "5 anti" campaigns. The first was aimed at eradicating the three vices of corruption, waste and bureaucracy; the five evils were bribery, tax evasion, theft of state property, cheating on government contracts and stealing information. At the time that these measures were undertaken, the private sector still accounted for 36 per cent of China's wholesale trade, 58 per cent of its retail trade, 39 per cent of its factory production and practically all of its agricultural production. But within a year most businessmen, terrorized in "struggle meetings," forced to "confess" illegal earnings, mistreatment of employees and evasion of taxes, were glad to be allowed to express publicly their joy in giving their businesses to "the people." The lucky ones were retained as managers and kept around for display purposes when foreign delegations came to town. Thousands of less fortunate "capitalists" were sent to labor camps where many were quite systematically worked to death.

The revolutionary measures were carried out by the Party ruthlessly and efficiently, following Mao's dictum: "A revolution is not the same as inviting people to dinner, or writing an essay or painting a picture. A revolution is an act of violence."

The violence was not limited to class enemies. The entire population was put through a process of ideological remolding, or brainwashing. In every village, factory and office "study meetings" were held where internal and foreign policies were discussed and interpreted, and active participation was demanded of all. There was no "freedom of silence." All were expected to confess any un-Maoist thoughts they may have had and to express their joy at having been freed from these evil remnants of the old regime.

While all this was going on, China became involved in a serious conflict in Korea. From the beginning, this war was described to the Chinese people as American aggression directed against China. Appealing to national patriotism in mass meetings, millions of Chinese were persuaded to "volunteer." The military authorities then chose units considered most appropriate for the campaign which raged for nearly two years. Throughout these operations the Chinese fought stubbornly and skillfully, and although the United Nations forces controlled both the sea and the air, the Chinese made a good showing. Even the Nationalist government in Taiwan expressed satisfaction that, after so many humiliating defeats, China could field an army that fought effectively against a Western force. The satisfaction of the Peking government was drastically diminished when, after the conclusion of a cease-fire in 1953, some fourteen thousand Chinese prisoners chose to go to Taiwan rather than return to their families under Communism on the Mainland.

Eventually, the Chinese economy made a remarkable recovery from its birth trauma, helped increasingly by the Soviet Union. In a new aid agreement in 1953 the Russians undertook the task of helping China build or rebuild a large number of enterprises, and Soviet technicians arrived in thousands, while thousands of Chinese workers and students went to the Soviet Union for various kinds of training. In a formal visit to Peking in 1954, Nikita Khrushchev promised even more aid and the return of Port Arthur and Dairen to China, as well as the abandonment of the Soviet economic concessions in Manchuria agreed upon in 1950.

Gaining confidence, the Peking government relaxed pressures on what was left of the "capitalists" and enlisted the cooperation of the entire population in massive movements to destroy rats, flies and sparrows, to build dams, dikes and canals, and to struggle against China's traditional illiteracy. At the same time, the government drew up plans for socialist industrialization.

The first move in this direction was agricultural collectivization—which began in 1953. Though the land technically remained privately owned and merely "contributed" to the cooperatives, tools and farm animals were pooled. Within two years, 125 million peasant households—96 per cent of all Chinese peasants—were collectivized. The way was made easier, of course, because the land reform had already destroyed the old village leadership and social structure and opened the way for Communist control. This is one reason why collectivization was more easily accomplished in China than it had been in the Soviet Union, where resistance was substantial until millions were starved into submission. In addition, each Chinese collective farmer was allowed to keep his own kitchen garden and a sow and a few chickens, and agricultural production did not decline, as it had in the Soviet Union.

Mao felt strong enough by 1955 to announce publicly his economic and social targets: preferential development of heavy industry as the basis for the further expansion of both agricultural and industrial production. To obtain the capital needed to expand China's old "treaty port" industry, labor productivity was to be increased far more rapidly than wages, while the peasantry was to be heavily taxed. The resources thus created were to expand the country's industrial capacity by roughly 100 per cent in five years, and 694 key industrial enterprises were to be built, of which the 156 largest would be designed and constructed by the Soviet Union.

Impressive results were achieved. By 1957, investments had soared, and so had production. The 1957 agricultural crop was twice that of 1949; light industrial production increased threefold; and heavy industrial production, tenfold.

The capital investments made in the Chinese economy from 1953 through 1957 amounted to about $18 billion compared to less than $500 million during the years from 1933-36. Most of this investment came from the Chinese themselves. Although Soviet credits paid for 31 per cent of the equipment and material for the 156 largest plants, these credits constituted only 3 per cent of total state investments during the five years. In line with Mao's policy, 58 per cent of these investments went into heavy industry and only 7.6 per cent into agriculture. Heavy industrial production increased rapidly. Rolled steel output increased from 1.1 million tons in 1952 to 4.5 million tons in 1957, coal from 63 to 130 million tons, power from 7 to 19 billion kilowatt-hours, cement from 3 to 7 million tons. China began producing automobiles, trucks, airplanes, machine tools, turbines.

China's trade also rose proportionately. During this period China managed to maintain a trade surplus, building up its foreign exchange reserves to about $500 million in 1957, and its national budget was kept in balance. There were major advances in science and in education at all levels. Despite the government's awkward indecision concerning what to do with China's unwieldy written language, enrollment in primary schools reached 90 million, and nearly half a million young people were enrolled in higher educational institutions, concentrating largely on science and technology.

Voices were raised in criticism of the fast pace of investment and development. "One cannot reach heaven in a single step," warned Vice President Chen Yun. Others pointed out that China's agriculture was catastrophically short of fertilizer. Many new industries were inoperative for lack of raw materials, power and transportation.

Disagreements among top party leadership may have been instrumental in the decision to allow a public blowing off of steam. In February, 1957, Mao made his famous statement: "Let a hundred flowers bloom, let a hundred schools of thought contend," apparently confident that the criticism would be positive, friendly and helpful. The results were unexpected, and from the Party's standpoint, shocking. Students and workers complained of party bureaucracy and poor leadership. Intellectuals protested against thought control; everyone complained of high prices and shortages of consumer goods. Strikes crippled some plants. Masses of peasants quit the newly organized collective farms. There was evidence of widespread loss of faith in Party leadership.

After only six weeks, the government clamped the lid back on and inaugurated a rectification campaign. During this campaign thousands who had raised their voices in protest or criticism were hustled off to prisons and labor camps. Three ministers and fifty members of the National People's Congress were dismissed. A handful were executed. Explained the *People's Daily:* "Serpents can be exterminated only when they are brought out into the open." To the people the lesson was clear: To avoid trouble, work hard; leave policy to the Party.

Dissension did not end, however. At a meeting of the People's Congress in June, 1957, Chou En-lai himself called for moderation and announced cuts in investment allocations for industry and construction, implying that food difficulties lay ahead. Other voices were raised in favor of relaxing the pressure on the peasants.

These criticisms were soon drowned out in a "torrent of Communist initiative," as Mao and Liu Shao-chi called for a new "Great Leap" of industrial and agricultural expansion.

They were motivated partially by increases in Soviet aid, which by mid-1957 reached a total of $2.4 billion. In addition, the Soviet breakthrough in missile and space technology at about this time may have persuaded Mao and his friends that the "inevitable"—world-wide victory of Communism—was at hand. Also important was the Russian promise to help the Chinese achieve their own atomic program, and the actual shipment of a small reactor, which was installed in Peking. Most important of all in motivating the new fervor for the "Great Leap" may have been Mao's realization that the Party was losing its leadership momentum, and that the only alternative to a slump was a massive surge forward.

Whatever other factors may have influenced the decision, the Party moved into the Great Leap in October, 1957. The first objective was an increase in agricultural production based on a new form of organization—the commune. There are different versions of the origin of the communes. According to the propaganda published by the *People's Daily*, the communes were "spontaneously started by the mass of the peasants on the basis of great socialist consciousness." The first commune was formed in Suiping county in Honan province. Hearing of it, so goes the official version, wise, kindly Chairman Mao went to see for himself. Lyrical stories tell how Mao moved knee-deep through the rice to talk to the enthusiastic peasants as they implored him to approve their commune. Housewives asked to be allowed to contribute their pots and pans to the commune mess hall, to turn their children over to the commune nursery so that they could work full time in the fields; young men pleaded for permission to drill in the militia before and after work. Finally Mao raised his hands over his head and proclaimed to the jubilant crowd: "Comrades! You have persuaded me. I pledge you that the Party will let you have your commune."

So much for the official story. Actually, Mao had mentioned the need for "communal ownership in socialist agriculture" as early as 1937. He returned to the theme in 1956 when he explained, "If we cannot jump from small-scale farming with animal-drawn implements to large-scale farming with machinery, we shall not be able to complete our socialist industrialization." During 1956 and 1957, several pilot communes were set up quietly in different provinces and carefully watched. By mid-1957, the imbalances of the rapidly expanding economy made it mandatory either to retrench or plunge boldly forward. Mao, already in his mid-60s, was no doubt anxious to see China industrialized in his lifetime. And Liu Shao-chi's militants had already drawn up the blueprints. The capital to continue the faltering industrialization program was to come from the villages—from the 15 billion workdays of labor unused in the slack farm seasons. Party leadership and mass psychology working through the communes would do the job. As Liu put it: "By relying on our huge population we soon can do anything within the realm of human possibility. Even without a large amount of modern equipment, a country of China's size can definitely build large modern enterprises and even attain unprecedented speed. In a short time industrial plants will dot every part of our country like stars in the sky."

When Mao swung his authority in the Party on Liu's side against the moderate group led by Chou En-lai, the decision was made. It was formally announced on August 28, 1958, and the immense Party machine went into operation. Enthusiastic cadres in every village called meetings, flayed the peasants with threats, urged them on with promises, to persuade them that the communes were their dearest wish. Within two months, more than 100 million peasant households were enrolled in 26,500 communes.

At the same time, birth control measures undertaken earlier in the year were quietly dropped, and attention was riveted on a program of human mobilization unseen since the building of the pyramids. The countryside was convulsed with movement. Tens of millions of men and women were marched off in military formation before

63

dawn every day to dig canals and dikes, clear land, build roads. French Professor Tibor Mende described one rural scene in 1959: "Endless lines of blue-clad men and women were filing up mountainsides like some unnatural stream changing its course. In the background, scattered all over the fields, multitudes of people were moving around with buckets on shoulder poles . . . reminding one of the rhythmic breathing of some mythological colossus, suddenly awakened and flexing its milliard muscles in a supreme effort to change the face of the earth."

Firecrackers, brass gongs, bugles and endless speeches kept the peasants at fever pitch as they were herded from field to construction job. With military precision, field kitchens and nurseries were organized to feed the adults and "emancipate" millions of women from their households and their children. Many private houses were pulled down, and the materials were used to build dormitories. The working day lengthened as the cadres goaded the members into demanding permission to work night and day for the Party.

In every commune, secondary projects were launched. The backyard blast furnaces were perhaps the most ambitious and the least useful. At one point in 1958, before leadership realized that much of the "iron" they produced was really nothing but slightly deoxidized iron ore and good for very little, more than half a million of these furnaces were in operation. They probably absorbed, during the period of the iron drive, a billion man days of labor, much of it badly needed in the fields. By the spring of 1959, the movement was left to peter out. The abandoned mud structures stood like silent witnesses to yet another demonic expenditure of human energy.

Visitors to communes in 1959 described a multitude of other shops and factories, sometimes using homemade wooden machinery, turning out toys, textiles, furniture and clothing, often for export at rock-bottom prices. Indian Professor S. Chandrasekhar visited one commune known as "the Commune of the Sixteen Guarantees," which were: food, clothing, housing, transportation to and from work, maternity benefits, medical care, care in old-age, funeral and burial, education, child care, recreation, a small wedding grant, twelve haircuts yearly, twenty baths annually, tailoring, and light. All these were available free to members, the Indian professor was told by the commune administration.

For all these projects the peasants were mobilized with military efficiency, led by squad commanders, carrying flags and banners, shouting oaths of allegiance and adoration for Mao and the Party. Platoons were driven to compete with one another in "labor emulation campaigns"; children over nine years of age were put to work weeding fields or carrying night soil "to learn productive habits"; and commune officials pushed so hard that at one point the *People's Daily* generously suggested, "The hours of shock production activities should not exceed two days and nights at a stretch." A refugee who reached Hong Kong about that time talked of working sixteen hours a day under "ordinary circumstances" and as long as twenty hours at a stretch when rice sprouts had to be transplanted.

The armed forces were mobilized for the Great Leap. In 1959, soldiers were put to work on 20,000 water conservation projects; 8,800 army trucks were used to help the country's faltering transportation system; and a total of 59 million man days of labor was thrown by the armed forces into the support of industrial and agricultural production. In 1960, a further 44 million man days were worked.

As the Great Leap gathered momentum, targets and production figures were increasingly exaggerated or even invented by Party zealots and others who felt forced to raise their figures lest they be thought lax. Accounting was thrown out. Statistics were solely to provide the needs of the Party. Said the head of the Statistical Bureau: "Statistics are not for statistics' sake (but) to urge progress and raise the backward. Chairman Mao gave us instructions that all systems hindering production must be rapidly corrected."

What happened—and what led to incredible claims of success—has been carefully analyzed by University of California economist Li Choh-ming. Falsification of statistics, he points out, largely resulted from the pressure to reach targets. Cadres and peasants were told "with finality" that application of Chairman Mao's "eight principles" for agriculture would produce miraculous yields, "provided only that proper leadership on the part of the cadres was forthcoming." When agricultural managers complained that fertilizer was in short supply, the Party leaders told them, "Make up for the shortage by deep plowing and close planting."

At the same time, in Peking, national production quotas were planned without any regard for reality. Unless a cadre was willing to run the risk of being branded a failure—or even worse, a "rightist"—he reported achievements equal to or above the target. At this news, Peking raised the target, which in turn prodded the cadre to inflate his claims, and so the statistics spiralled away.

Production claims were extraordinary. Pig iron output in 1959, said Chou En-lai, was 13.6 million tons, a 131 per cent increase over 1957's 5.9 million tons; steel production was 11 million tons, a 107 per cent increase over 1957's 5.3 million tons; coal production had also more than doubled to 270 million tons. Motor vehicle production of 7,500 units in 1957 rose to 16,000 in 1958. And so it went.

Intellectuals were drafted into the struggle and produced inspirational poems, like this one:

> Chairman Mao:
> points to a mountain, trees grow tall,
> points to a river, the water runs clear,
> draws a line on the map on the wall
> and roads and railroads appear. . . .

The Great Leap affected schools and colleges. When Indian Professor Chandrasekhar visited the Shanghai Academy of Social Sciences (formerly St. John's University) in 1959, he remarked to the vice-director conducting him around the campus that there did not seem to be many students. Well, he was told, of the 5,000 registered students, 2,000 were working in Shanghai factories, but they took courses "once a week"; another 2,000 were working on farms in the Shanghai area and they would come back to their studies in a year or two when the country's temporary food problems were solved; 200 were on steel duty, and another 200 were on maneuvers with the militia on the Fukien front. Visiting another university, the Indian demographer found that examinations were suspended for the time being, as was the granting of degrees.

During two summer weeks in July, 1959, according to the Honan *Peasants' Daily,* 367,000 peasants collapsed, and 29,000 died in the fields of Honan. Other reports indicated 7,000 died in the fields of Kiangsi, 8,000 in Kiangsu, and 13,000 in Chekiang.

All this had an effect on the armed forces, many of whose peasant members "did not clearly understand certain questions of socialist change," to quote an official explanation. A military shake-up was ordered. Out went old revolutionary Marshal Peng Te-huai; in came Lin Piao, with former security chief Lo Jui-ching as Chief of Staff. The new leadership introduced the "month-in-the-ranks" program for all officers.

In December, 1958, Party leadership met in Wuhan to take stock of the situation. From this meeting the ambiguous slogan "Walk on Two Legs" emerged, an admonition, appropriately simplified for the masses, to develop industry and agriculture simultaneously. Finally, in August, 1959, at a secret Central Committee meeting at Lushan, it fell to Premier Chou—who had preached caution all along—to do more humiliating backtracking. He explained, "Because of the lack of experience in estimating output under the unprecedented bumper conditions of 1958" and "because of lack of proper allocation of the labor force . . . the work of reaping, threshing, gathering and storing was so poorly done that some part of the harvest was lost." Chou thereupon scaled down production claims drastically. Instead of the announced 375 million tons of grain in 1958, only 270 million tons were produced, he said. (Actually, it is estimated by experts that food grain output could not have been more than about 193 million tons in that year.) This confession was followed by a diatribe against "a very small number of people who remain apathetic to our country's great achievements . . . and even try hard to spread their extremely erroneous ideas. . . . Those who assert that the people's communes are in 'an awful mess' are none other

67

than the imperialists who are violently hostile to our country's socialistic cause."

Nationwide food shortages forced further revisions. At the eighth plenary session of the Central Committee, Premier Chou admitted the 1958 industrial statistics had also been faulty. From the 11 million tons of steel claimed, 3 million produced in the native furnaces were deducted. The claim for pig iron was reduced from 13.6 million tons to 9.5 million.

In the crucial area of agricultural products, the cotton claim of 3.3 million tons, a 101 per cent increase over 1957's 1.6 million tons, was reduced to 2.1 million, only a 28 per cent increase over 1957. The livestock claims were modest, a 6 per cent gain in large animals, 17 per cent in sheep and goats. In the important export area of hogs, the original claim of 180 million was reduced to 160 million, only a 10 per cent increase over 1957.

The embarrassing scaling down and public admission of statistical errors also forced revisions of 1959 targets to lower levels. The 1959 steel target was revised from 18 to 12 million tons. The "iron" produced by village furnaces rusting on the ground was plain for all to see.

The Communists simply could not hide the harsh realities in agriculture. No amount of ideological wizardry could conjure up food. At the same time that hunger pangs struck, China was suffering from a bad case of economic indigestion. Only a vast re-emphasis on agriculture could remedy it.

China's peasants were apparently expected to accept the massive revision of targets and claims as they accepted other natural phenomena over which they had no control. For the intelligentsia, however, whose memories might be expected to create inhibitions, the Party made appropriate provisions. Said the *People's Daily:* "Revolutions are necessarily confused. And those opposed to errors are also opposed to the revolution. In new experiences mistakes cannot be avoided. . . ."

The 1959 crop, according to the best estimates, was about 167 million tons of food grain—down 14 per cent from the 1958 bumper crop. This reduced the diet of the average Chinese to below 2,000 calories a day. Food queues were common. Worse was to come.

The Russians had been skeptical of the Great Leap from its beginning. They stated publicly that they thought the communes were "forty years too early" and Chinese planning irresponsible and hysterical. But they did not interfere. When the Chinese began to criticize the Soviet policies in Poland and Hungary as weak and indecisive, however, and to appeal to the fledgling nations of Africa and Asia to follow the Chinese path in a mighty shortcut to socialism, the Russians withdrew their support from China. The first indication was the repudiation in June, 1959, of the Soviet commitment to help China's nuclear program. In the summer of 1960, a far greater blow fell when the Russians summarily withdrew at least ten thousand technicians from Chinese industry and backed out of further aid deliveries, while insisting that China pay both the interest and the principal provided for in the previous agreements.

This problem is the subject of the next chapter. It is important to know that these Soviet actions constituted an important factor in forcing Mao and his government into the humiliating "Great Retreat" during the hungry years of 1960 and 1961.

The Great Retreat is a sorry chapter in Chinese history. In agriculture the disaster involved a drastic drop in food grain tonnage. The government blamed the weather, which was sub-normal, but not enough to account for the decline. Other factors were the diversion of labor from agriculture to other activities, waste and the cumulative frustration and fatigue of farmers daily roused before dawn by commune gongs and marched off as "volunteer" labor to the neglect of the fields.

Still another factor was that the communes themselves were too large to support the highly developed and delicately balanced horticulture through which millions of Chinese farmers had nursed a living from their tiny patches of land over the centuries. Take the example of one farmer in Kwangtung province: A few mulberry trees fed silk worms, whose cocoons brought in a small cash income; the residue of this operation was then fed to fish in a pond to put some protein in the diet made up essentially of grain grown in the next field, fertilized by night soil, and tenderly cultivated with small tools which lasted for years or even generations. Such units fed millions of Chinese families except in bad years, when they starved. Suddenly in 1959, commune leadership ordered the mulberry trees cut down to make charcoal for a local blast furnace; people were ordered away to dig a canal when they should have been plowing. The old farmers objected, and were silenced by the activists who talked glibly of making up for the loss of labor by using deep plowing and close planting, and through the use of chemical fertilizers. The first two practices turned out to be disastrous, and were discontinued in late 1960. As for chemical fertilizer, China produced only about 2 million tons in 1960 and needed at least fifteen times that amount to bring China's yields up to the level of Japan's.

It was in this climate that the government faced its Great Retreat in agriculture. During the late months of 1960 and most of 1961, the government, realizing that the communes were doing more harm than good, so modified the commune system that by the end of 1961 little remained of it but the name. In the first place, the brigade, about a thousand workers, replaced the much larger communes as the unit of organization in China's agriculture. This unit was broken up during 1961 into the smaller production team, usually a village, of from sixty to a hundred workers. The Party ordered respect for the wisdom of the old farmers and warned against taking needed agricultural labor for secondary activities. More important, members were to be permitted to produce food of their own by cultivating small garden plots or a few fruit trees beside their homes, or raising fowl and domestic animals. By late 1961, the individual plots amounted to perhaps 5 per cent of the total sown area and by 1964 were producing 14 per cent of the country's farm output. The products of the private gardens could be eaten or sold at market prices.

Individual commune members were allowed again to own their own homes and other possessions, including small farm tools, bicycles, radios, watches, furniture, and even bank deposits. The sixteen- and eighteen-hour days were condemned by the government which ordered respect for a "normal" workday that might average ten hours during busy seasons. Parents were given back the authority to decide about their children's education and place of residence. Although communal mess halls were still recommended, they were no longer compulsory.

Peking continued its strategic retreat into 1962. It was not enough for leadership to recognize that the commune system had failed, that collective responsibility was no responsibility, and without effective responsibility agriculture could not be productive. The government also had to re-establish the prestige and image of China's oldest unit of responsibility—the family. This procedure must have been wrenching to cadres who had worked so hard during the Great Leap to break down family ties and loyalties. But the necessity was clear and compelling. Families had to be urged to look after their own, to accept and integrate the millions of demobilized proletarians back into family village units, feed them until they could begin feeding themselves. So the country's huge propaganda machine had to undertake the task in a manner that would avoid an admission of error. Here is one of countless examples of how they went about it: On May 12, 1962, the Peking newspaper *Chung-kuo Ching-nien Pao* (China Youth News) ran the following letter:

Comrade Editor:

I remember that two months ago I read in your paper an article on filial piety. It was stressed in the article that it was "compulsory and dutiful" for a son or daughter to support his or her parents. I was greatly enlightened after I had read that article.

But, in a family, there are the parents and their children, as well as their daughters-in-law. Of course, a daughter-in-law is not the daughter of her father- and mother-in-law. For this reason, a daughter-in-law may dislike her father- and mother-in-law and does not show sufficient respect for them. She may even quarrel often with them and want to leave them. On certain occasions when her husband shows greater concern for the well-being of his parents, she may also quarrel with him. Comrade editor, is a daughter-in-law obliged to support her father- and mother-in-law? Please enlighten me.

Wang Tung-an of Houying Commune
Liaocheng, Shantung

In the same issue the editor's answer was published.

Comrade Wang Tung-an:

It is "compulsory and dutiful" for a daughter-in-law to respect and support her father- and mother-in-law, as it is for a son or daughter to do so for his parents. If a daughter-in-law refuses to support her father- and mother-in-law under the excuse that she is not their daughter and even tries to urge her husband to live away from his parents so that he may avoid the duty of supporting his parents, that will be wrong and improper. *It is a general practice for parents to feed their young children and for children to support their parents when their parents are old.* In our socialist big family, we should observe this practice better than it was observed in the past. We should make the older generation feel more the warmth brought to them by the new society and should not be cold to them. If some people in the old society could give warmth to their parents, while we in the new society want to forsake and refuse to take care of our parents, we should be acting contrary to our morality and such conduct would not be permitted in our new society . . .

Liu Wen-ting

In industry, the Great Leap was clearly faltering by the end of 1959, but Peking leadership, lost in its increasingly fictitious figures, announced blandly that the essential targets of the second Five-Year Plan were being fulfilled three years ahead of schedule. They made modest claims for coal and machine tools produced during this period, and promised immense increases for 1960. But as officialdom gradually admitted, some of the coal was in reality rocks and dirt, much of the cement was hardly cement at all, and much of the steel was known to be of inferior quality. Furthermore, as Peking admitted, light industrial production was definitely behind schedule. Finally, as top leadership was beginning to understand, the frantic human energy of the Great Leap was running down, and machinery used twenty-four hours a day without proper maintenance, was also collapsing. Huge imbalances were developing in the complex interlocking plans for production and delivery of materials, equipment and parts.

The Peking leadership now made a fundamental and shocking decision: slow down on industrialization in favor of agricultural development. The decision was announced by planner Li Fu-chun. In his 1960 report, Li called on industry to support agriculture. Allocations of steel and machinery for agricultural use were sharply increased over the previous year. He demanded the forced production of fertilizers and major efforts on the creation of seventeen large and 140 small chemical fertilizer plants. He also called for an increase in capital investment in the transport and communications network which, he said, "cannot at present keep pace with industrial and agricultural production and the circulation of commodities."

The population knew, without being told by Li, that the economy was in imbalance. Food and cloth rationing had begun in the last quarter of 1959, and in early 1960 the rice ration was cut. Workers were urged to grow sweet potatoes in their yards and raise their own chickens and pigs. As diet deteriorated, absenteeism increased because of sickness or because of the workers' gardening activities. Massive shortages of raw materials began to plague plant after plant. In an attempt to revive failing incentives, the government reinstated piecework. But transport shortfalls and shortages of coal cut production levels in many parts of the country.

Then, in the summer of 1960, Soviet technicians were withdrawn. As machines were shut down by breakdowns, other production units and their personnel were idled for lack of materials. The government reacted with what in retrospect seems a rather hysterical measure: the sending of an estimated 20 million workers, particularly from small marginal factories, back to the villages to work the land.

Production figures for 1960 were never announced. Peking also failed to announce targets for 1961 or production for that year. The People's Congress did not meet in 1961, although the Central Committee is thought to have had a secret meeting in September in Hangchow. In February, 1962, the *People's Daily* referred to 1962 as "a year of adjustment." Industrial production was admittedly falling. The question was when it would hit bottom.

The Great Retreat in industry introduced into China's economy psychological factors not unlike those at work in a snowballing recession in a capitalist economy. Ma-

73

chines were shut down because of anticipated shortages of raw materials, thereby causing actual shortages for other machines. Leadership probably fell into some disarray, though there is no evidence of actual strife. The planners who had opposed the Great Leap from the beginning came back into positions of authority, replacing the dogmatists who had so clearly failed. Orders went out to relax the pressures on the harassed workers. Wrote Po I-po: "It is wrong to think merely of production and not of the life of the people, to neglect the harmony between work and rest . . . to eat up reserves, to use equipment and manpower to excess. . . ." Wise old Chairman Mao was quoted as having said all along, "Food for men is like oil for machines." There had been talk about overtaking and surpassing Britain in ten or fifteen years. This was changed to forty or fifty years. Said planner Li Fu-chun soberly: "There are many arduous years ahead before China can be made a rich industrial state."

The situation continued to deteriorate. An engineer from a North China cement plant stated that in the first few months of 1961, seven out of eight mills closed down for lack of materials and labor. Forty per cent of the plant's workers were sick or weak, and 30 per cent were sent to the villages to help agriculture. After June, the one operating mill stopped making cement but began processing grass, roots, and other vegetable material into ersatz flour.

The best estimates are that some 20 million more workers were sent back to the farms in 1961, and the movement continued in 1962 though probably at a decreasing rate. But altogether during the next thirty months, at least 40 million urban workers were ordered back to crowded and hungry villages to grub and forage as best they could. For second- or third-generation city dwellers, who had no village to go back to, the impact of this experience was traumatic. Though the political consequences of this exodus may be delayed, in the long run they will probably be as important as the actual closing down of thousands of shops and factories.

From bits and pieces of information in the Chinese Communist press, we see Peking's admissions of catastrophic shortfalls. A large number of articles complained of inefficiency and even corruption among the Party cadres, many of whom seemed unable or unwilling to accept the fragmentation of the communes into brigades and work teams, but insisted on maintaining their central offices where they "wallow in conferences," to use the *People's Daily* phrase. One example cited was a Party branch secretary in Kwangsi province who in one month ran fourteen conferences which occupied his full time for 14½ days in addition to thirteen other simultaneous conferences on the brigade level. Other reports cited cadres who occupied themselves largely with supplementary industries and "live privileged lives apart from the masses." The *People's Daily* attacked cadres who, "blind to reality, recklessly chased after a high production target."

The results of China's crisis were acknowledged officially on the highest level. In January, 1961, Li Fu-chun, Chairman of the State Planning Commission, said: "The whole nation must concentrate on strengthening the agricultural front . . . In heavy industry . . . capital construction must be appropriately reduced." The Peking press referred several times to the calamitous results of a "comparatively low food ration," and in October, 1961, the *People's Daily* admitted: "The grave natural calamities which occurred for three successive years between 1959 and 1961 have resulted in a reduction of agricultural production. The reduction in the output of grain, industrial crops and subsidiary rural products has affected the production of both light and heavy industry, and consequently commodity supplies and the people's livelihood."

And the Chinese people were aware of what was going on. In 1962 many transcripts of interviews with refugees from various parts of China dealt with the refugees' answers to the question, "Why did you flee?" There were references to hunger or the fear of hunger, overwork, and arbitrary administration. But the most frequently heard single reason was, "I do not want to work for the Communists any more."

The Great Retreat left a heavy mark on China's domestic and foreign trade. In 1961 alone, the country's foreign trade fell 25 per cent. Most of China's exports were being used to pay the Russians—more than $250 million a year—and to pay the Canadians and Australians for food imports, without which millions of Chinese would have starved. Domestic trade also languished as nearly everything fell under rigid rationing, and prices on unrationed items like vegetables and "free" eggs rose to astronomical levels.

The effect was exceedingly harsh on China's foreign exchange reserves which fell from about $300 million at the beginning of 1960 to about $100 million in early 1962—shockingly close to bankruptcy.

As the Great Retreat ended with relative stabilization in 1962, the experts in Hong Kong tried to draw up a balance sheet for the Chinese economy at that time. It looked like this:

The position of Chinese agriculture was serious, but not catastrophic. The Chinese people were hungry, not starving. Thanks to imports and an effective rationing system, mass starvation in the immediate future was unlikely.

The state of Chinese industry, on the other hand, was catastrophic. The industrialization plans around which the government had woven its policies had, in effect, been abandoned. Between 30 and 50 million urban workers had been sent back to their villages, and industrial production was at least 30 per cent below the levels of 1958 and probably still falling. Imports of capital equipment had ceased, except for chemical fertilizer machinery and atomic development equipment. China's foreign exchange reserves were at rock bottom. A Soviet debt moratorium would have helped, but the Russians made no move in this direction, and the Chinese were too proud—or too astute—to make the request.

Though no serious rifts had appeared on the surface in Chinese political leadership and no rebellions had plagued the regime, except in distant Tibet, every evidence indicated a dangerous degree of popular discontent in many parts of China. There was a strong probability of deep disagreement at the top about the wisdom of the leadership which had led more than half a billion people through the economic and human cataracts of the Great Leap and the Great Retreat.

5. THE SINO-SOVIET CONFLICT

On February 14, 1950, four months after they founded the People's Republic in Peking, the Chinese Communists signed a "Sino-Soviet Treaty of Friendship, Alliance and Mutual Assistance." Said Chairman Mao Tse-tung: "Everybody sees that the unity of the two great countries, China and the Soviet Union, sealed by solemn treaty, will be lasting and indestructible."

On the tenth anniversary of the treaty in 1960, Chairman Mao and his top lieutenants—Liu Shao-chi, Chu Teh and Chou En-lai—sent a congratulatory message to the then Soviet Premier Nikita Khrushchev, reaffirming that the treaty formalized an unbreakable fraternal relationship which no force could destroy. "The Chinese," the message said, "regard the consolidation and development of the unity of China and the Soviet Union, and of the socialist camp headed by the Soviet Union, as their most sacred international obligation."

The picture changed drastically during the next seven years. Although the treaty still exists on paper, there is no sign of friendship or alliance or mutual assistance between the two Communist giants. On the contrary, Communist China and the Soviet Union are in open disagreement on many major issues. Peking, moreover, has long since denied Moscow's leadership of the world socialist camp. "The Communist Party of China and the Communist Party of the Soviet Union are equal," declared the Chinese Party's Central Committee as early as 1963.

All through 1966 and into 1967, the two governments hurled insults at each other, while their troops exchanged shots across their long frontier.

Yet Moscow and Peking pay homage to the same deities and embrace systems of ideological belief so nearly identical that it takes a specialist to identify the differences.

There are several areas of Sino-Soviet conflict: historic, economic, political, racial and ideological.

HISTORIC ENMITY. As we saw in Chapter I, even in antiquity raiders from the north and west harassed the early agricultural society created by the Chinese along the coasts and in the river valleys. Many of these raiders came from areas that now constitute Soviet territory—Siberia, Kazakhstan, perhaps farther west. These incursions so disturbed the Chinese that they built one of the world's most impressive military defenses, the Great Wall, for protection.

Later the direction of the attacks changed, and from the early centuries of our era down through the fifteenth century, invaders based in lands now part of China— Attila, and the Great Khans, down through Tamburlaine— swept westward, some of them as far as the Danube and the Rhine, and all passed through Russia. For two centuries, Russia suffered under the Tartar yoke. To this century, Russian mothers frighten naughty children with the threat, "If you don't behave, the Chinese will get you."

In addition to this ancient enmity, territorial disputes of more recent origin divide the two nations. For centuries during the Han Dynasty and again under the Mings and Manchus, China had asserted its suzerainty over much of what is now Soviet Central Asia, over all the Maritime Province, and much of eastern Siberia. In the eighteenth and nineteenth centuries, an aggressive Czarist empire pushed eastward and seized these lands from a China preoccupied with defense against other enemies. These conquests were formulated in a series of treaties which the Chinese agreed to under duress.

Later the Russians pushed even farther—occupying Port Arthur, Harbin, Mukden and parts of Manchuria. These latter areas were ceremoniously returned to China in 1949. But the Chinese now demand much more. They demand a review of the shotgun treaties of the eighteenth and nineteenth centuries and a return to China of some 410,000 square miles of Soviet territory—an area the size of Western Europe. For example, on May 17, 1966, China's Foreign Minister Chen Yi told a group of visiting Scandinavian journalists: "The Russian thieves annexed 1,500,000 square kilometers of Chinese territory including land occupied in the nineteenth century and also areas seized in breach of treaties since. . . ."

No Russian government, Soviet or any other, could agree to give up these areas. The Russian people, both before and since the revolution, have invested great wealth and effort in these lands. They have built great cities—Vladivostok and Alma Ata—and railroads and factories and dams. The population of these provinces, once largely Asian, is now predominantly Russian. This territorial conflict, based in history, cannot easily be resolved.

The historic enmities and territorial disputes alone would be ample reason for conflict between China and the Soviet Union, even if no other issues were outstanding. But other issues are present.

ECONOMIC CONFLICT. China's huge population lives in a country whose arable lands and minerals, power, and forest resources are far less than those of the Soviet Union, whose population is a third of China's. Over the past half-century, the Soviet population has been increasing annually by only about 0.6 per cent on the average, or by a total of about 50 million. With its current officially-estimated 2 per cent increase rate, China's population grows by 50 million every three or four years. Soviet per capita Gross National Product is currently about twelve times that of China. It has been estimated that Red China's GNP in 1966 was only a trifle more than it was ten years earlier. But her population has increased by about 100 million during the decade, so the income per person has been reduced. The Soviet Union's productive forces, something always watched carefully by Marxists, are today infinitely superior to China's. China has only about 120,000 tractors and trucks; the Soviet Union has millions of both. Russians are shod; Chinese are barefoot. Russians eat well enough; Chinese are hungry. Most important, the Soviet Union has remote yet vast, rich areas whose forests, minerals and fields are virtually untapped.

Only an arbitrary frontier 4,500 miles long separates the two countries. China's other neighbors—Afghanistan, India, Vietnam, Korea—are poor themselves, and are separated from China by mountains. Only Laos and Burma are underpopulated and fairly accessible. Far and away the best "pickings" lie to the north and west. The Soviet people realize this. Soviet high school students have told the author: "We shall have trouble with the Chinese. They are numerous and diligent and very poor. It has happened before and may well happen again."

This inequality between the Chinese and Russian resources, this close proximity of poverty and wealth, forms the background for the economic relations, and the economic conflict between the two nations.

Before the Communists overran the Chinese mainland in 1949, China's economic relations with the Soviet Union had been limited. During World War II, the Russians were far too preoccupied in Europe to develop any trade with the embattled Nationalist Chinese, and by Stalin's own choice had little official commerce with the Chinese Communists in their Yenan fortress.

In 1945, before the smoke of battle had cleared, the Russians moved into Manchuria, routed the already defeated Japanese in a five-day "war," with the hope of playing a major role in East Asia and the Western Pacific. While they failed in this, they did manage to make off with an estimated $2 billion worth of industrial equipment and other booty from the Manchurian industrial center the Japanese had spent twenty years building. They also seized Japanese weapons and gave some of them to the Chinese Communists. The Soviet reparations program in Germany was poorly organized, and much equipment rusted away to uselessness or was lost. But in Manchuria the program was even less well-organized, partly because the Russians had no nearby industrial areas where such machinery could be used. Thousands of tons of valuable equipment were dragged off just over the Soviet frontier where much of it stayed until it was valueless. Some of it was sent back to China in the early 1950s as Soviet economic aid.

During the late 1940s, the Russians were preoccupied with the rehabilitation of their own economy, and no economic contacts worth mentioning developed with China. But then came the Chinese Communist victory in 1949, and with it the initiation of major economic relations between the Soviet Union and China in the form of trade, with economic, military and technical aid.

In fact, soon after the founding of the Chinese People's Republic, its trade with the Soviet Union grew steadily at the expense of Japan and the West. Red China's total foreign trade grew from about $1.8 billion in 1950 to more than $5 billion by 1960, of which 80 per cent was with the Communist bloc, mainly the Soviet Union. (See Appendix I for more details.) But due to the subsequent Sino-Soviet dispute, trade between the two countries dropped drastically, by as much as 70 per cent between 1959 and 1963, according to official Soviet figures. Simultaneously, the Sino-Soviet dispute caused European and Japanese manufacturers to scramble for the "China market" to fill the gap caused by the disruption of Sino-Soviet trade. Japanese Foreign Office sources estimate that Sino-Soviet trade volume, which was $2 billion in 1959, decreased to $420 million in 1965, and has fallen even lower since, though no figures have been published.

Naturally, Peking and Moscow blamed each other for the downward trend of the Sino-Soviet trade. After the rift broke into the open in July, 1963, *Pravda* charged that the Chinese were creating an economic split in the Communist world by advocating a "go-it-alone" policy. They charged that the Chinese were utilizing the policy of "self-reliance" to "sabotage" the COMECON (Council for Mutual Economic Aid) and to play on national fears and sensitivities. In other words, the Russians thought that the Chinese were being "nationalistic" and "schismatic."

The Communist Chinese disagreed. They charged Moscow: "You have used trade between our countries to bring political pressure to bear . . . the prices of many of the goods we imported . . . were much higher than those on the world market." Peking also claimed that the main reason for the weakening of economic ties was the brutal Soviet decision to withdraw their technicians in July, 1960, which "inflicted incalculable difficulties and losses on China's economy, national defense and scientific research." According to a *People's Daily* editorial of December 4, 1963, the Soviet authorities in July, 1960, "Suddenly unilaterally decided to withdraw all the experts who were assisting our country in its work, to tear up 343 agreements and supplementary provisions." The Russian withdrawal, plus Moscow's refusal to grant China any debt moratorium, seriously aggravated China's economic difficulties and put pressure on her dangerously low foreign exchange reserves.

One of China's key problems during this period was the drop in agricultural production which caused a decline in her exports. The sharpest decreases were in rice, soybeans, peanuts, meat, eggs, and edible oils. Some detailed figures in the downward trend of the Sino-Soviet trade appear in Table I in the Appendix.

During the peak year of 1959, 49 per cent of Red China's foreign trade was conducted with the Soviet Union. But as Sino-Soviet relations worsened year after year, Peking diverted her foreign trade to Western countries and Japan. By 1963, Sino-Soviet trade had decreased to 22 per cent of China's total. In 1966, the ratio dropped even lower—to a mere 9 per cent. For more details see Table II and Table III in the Appendix.

The grinding poverty and general plight of the Chinese people during the 1960s are well known. That the Soviet Union did not see fit to offer any debt moratorium, but squeezed the Chinese unmercifully, forcing them to service their debt and repay principal literally out of the mouths of the hungry Chinese people—indicates the measure of Moscow's hostility.

That the Chinese paid—a total of about $2.3 billion at the rate of almost half a billion dollars a year during the early 1960s, finally liquidating their indebtedness in 1966—is a tribute to the fanatical pride and drive of the Chinese.

That the Chinese, during this difficult period, initiated and sustained a foreign aid program of their own is truly extraordinary. This program is an economic expression of the Sino-Soviet conflict. So intensely do the Chinese leaders feel their competitive relationship with the Russians that they find it necessary, under the most difficult circumstances, to commit several hundred million dollars in economic and military aid both to other socialist states and to remote bourgeois or even feudal states like Cambodia and Yemen.

POLITICAL CONFLICTS. Political disagreements between the Chinese and Russian Communists date back to 1921 when the Moscow-based, Russian-oriented Comintern took the initiative in organizing the Chinese Communist Party (CPC), one of whose founders was Mao Tse-tung. From the beginning, the Comintern leaders were convinced of the necessity of basing Communist activities on the working class rather than on the peasantry or on other sectors of the population. So they urged the CPC to collaborate with or even temporarily to join the Kuomintang, the revolutionary-nationalist party under Dr. Sun Yat-sen's leadership. For the Kuomintang did have strong roots, not only among China's Nationalists, but also among the young working class communities which had grown up around the textile industry of Shanghai, the coal mines of Manchuria, and other infant industries of awakening China.

The Soviet government tried to guide the CPC by summoning Chinese leaders to Moscow periodically and through its "representative," as the resident political agent of the Comintern in the various countries was called. At that time, the most important Comintern representative in China was Mikhail Borodin, who took the blame for the collapse of the Canton Commune in 1927. He was shunted off to the editorship of the Moscow *Daily News* and finally died in an East Siberian concentration camp in 1952. Another was V. Lominadze, a huge, near-sighted Georgian who, after the debacle in China in 1927, stumbled into the "Right-Left Bloc" in the late 1920s and was sent in semi-disgrace as Secretary of the Magnitogorsk Party Committee in Siberia until his suicide in 1936. Earl Browder, later General Secretary of the U.S. Communist Party, was also active in China in the mid-1920s, particularly in attempts to capture for the CPC the leadership of the Chinese trade union movement.

Stalin, by various means, used the CPC in his struggle with Trotsky, forcing his Chinese comrades into the trap set in 1927 by Chiang Kai-shek. On April 12, 1927, Chiang launched his anti-Communist coup, effectively destroying or dispersing Communist organizations in Shanghai and Nanking. Moscow refused to believe that the Kuomintang could not be utilized, and continued to insist on collaboration until the Chinese Communist Party was driven underground. Mao Tse-tung, then already a top-ranking leader, was attacked by Moscow as a deviationist because of his refusal to follow Moscow's instructions. He led remnants of the organization into the rural areas of Kiangsi province where, in relative isolation from both the Chinese proletariat and the vindictive terror of the Kuomintang, he organized the first Chinese Soviet Republic. Though scoffed at by Moscow as a mere peasant assemblage, Mao's organization formed the nucleus of the effective Eighth Route Army, which was to become China's victorious People's Liberation Army. Mao resisted Moscow's attempts to persuade him to submit to "proletarian leadership," or to risk all on a frontal attack on the Kuomintang-held cities. And he emerged strong enough to lead his forces on the historic Long March to distant Yenan in China's northwest.

Throughout this period, Mao and such collaborators as Chu Teh and Chou En-lai were repeatedly criticized by the Russians, but they managed always to avoid a rupture and formal expulsion. They remained persistently Chinese in their policies. They resented bitterly the Soviet Party leaders' erroneous analysis and bull-headed policies. On the basis of these early attempts of the Russians to sacrifice the Chinese Party to Soviet interests, Mao's later insistence on maintaining his independence of action and his refusal to subordinate himself to Moscow on important issues become understandable.

The most charitable interpretation of Moscow's actions toward the CPC for the first quarter-century of its existence is that Moscow leaders seemed incapable of understanding the revolutionary processes in under-developed, Oriental lands with predominantly peasant populations who associated colonialism with white men from Europe. Today, racism has been made an issue by both sides in the Sino-Soviet dispute. Peking has sought to keep the Russians out of Afro-Asian conferences because the Russians are white, and the Chinese have not seemed reluctant to use this racism shamelessly, playing on the prejudices of the Africans particularly, although numerous cases of Chinese discrimination against Negro students in China are on the record. The Russians have not hesitated to discuss the "yellow menace," though this has not been incorporated into the Soviet Union's official policy. Official and unofficial Russians often express disgust at the intolerable egocentricity of the Chinese, who assume their own superiority is so axiomatic as to require no proof, or even formal expression.

As early as 1946, top Chinese Communist theoretician Liu Shao-chi claimed that Mao Tse-tung had created an Asian form of Marxism and that he had analyzed and solved the problems facing the semi-feudal, semi-colonial countries in a Chinese way. Thus, Chinese Communist leadership had already placed Mao on a level with Marx and Lenin, rather than with Stalin.

After the establishment of the People's Republic of China, Moscow hastened to repudiate the special privileges it had enjoyed in China since Czarist days. It withdrew its naval base from Port Arthur and turned over to the Chinese Communists its installations there and at Dairen. It acknowledged Manchuria as an integral part of China and renounced its half interest in the Manchurian railway system. From then on, political and economic relations between Peking and Moscow were normal. High-level visits were exchanged, and Moscow extended economic aid. There is little doubt, however, that the Russians were irritated by the Chinese claim that Mao's theories on revolution constituted an original ideology and that "Mao's road" was the one to be followed by other underdeveloped countries, particularly in Asia and Africa. When Stalin died in 1953, Mao allowed Party associates to declare him the world's top Communist, the greatest contemporary theoretician of Marxism-Leninism. But no major issue arose to test Mao until the Twentieth Congress of the Russian Party in February, 1956. It was here that bitter discord flared into public expression.

At this Congress Premier Nikita Khrushchev came up with several major reappraisals of Marxist-Leninist theory.

He presented peaceful coexistence between Communism and Capitalism as a "fundamental principle," because the only alternative would be the most destructive war of history. War was not inevitable, because new social forces made possible peaceful evolution to socialism in many capitalist countries. Though the Chinese did not challenge this thesis and its implications until two years later, they began thinking of Khrushchev and his colleagues as "revisionists" who betrayed the revolution out of fear of war. The issue of de-Stalinization was also raised by Khrushchev at the Twentieth Congress in his famous "letter," and in his criticisms of Stalin from the floor of the Congress. Peking leaders began reproaching Khrushchev for airing Stalin's crimes as constituting, in effect, an attack against Communism itself. The Chinese were further disturbed by Khrushchev's implied denunciation of Mao as a practitioner of the cult of personality. Finally, the Chinese foresaw that Khrushchev's attack on Stalin would unleash immense and destructive forces throughout the Communist world. And, indeed, not many months passed before crises in Hungary and Poland erupted, a number of leaders like Italy's Togliatti began talking of "polycentrism," and mass defections shook the Communist parties of the West.

Since then, the relationship between China and the Soviet Union has never been the same. Although Peking supported Moscow after the Hungarian rebellion in October, 1956, and although Chinese and Soviet leaders agreed on a political truce during the Twenty-first Congress of the Soviet Party in February, 1959—the *detente* lasted hardly six months. By the end of the year, Peking and Moscow were exchanging propaganda broadsides again. The showdown between the two protagonists came during the "Congress of 81" in Moscow in November, 1960, when the world Communist camp was split between pro-Peking and pro-Moscow factions.

It was in this climate that the Sino-Soviet dispute on global strategy erupted. Mao's assertions were based on his conviction that the "east wind" was now predominant over the "west wind," and on the "overwhelming superiority of the socialist forces to the imperialist forces." Mao needled the Soviet Union, which had succeeded in testing its first intercontinental ballistic missiles, to make a bold offensive against their common "imperialist enemy." The Russians demurred, arguing that coexistence between two separate systems was a form of the class struggle, and that new weapons made coexistence not only possible but necessary. By November, 1962, the Sino-Soviet political conflict had become so bitter and overt that *Hung Chi* (Red Flag), theoretical journal of the Chinese Communist Party, editorially called on Communists everywhere to unite to combat the revisionist views of the Soviet Government.

During the following years relations worsened as both sides used flagrant expressions to attack each other in "open letters." When, in October, 1964, Khrushchev was ousted from the Soviet premiership, Peking was jubilant. A *People's Daily* editorial of November 7 described his fall as "a very good thing," and for a while the Chinese Communists were hopeful of a new Soviet line more to their liking. But they were soon disappointed, and accused the new Soviet leadership of practicing "Khrushchev revisionism without Khrushchev." Khrushchev's policies remained in force: de-Stalinization, U.S.-Soviet cooperation, the partial nuclear test ban, peaceful transition to socialism, the supply of military aid to India, preparations for an international Communist meeting, etc.

The Sino-Soviet political dispute continues to this day. In fact, the gap has become wider since the launching of the "Proletarian Cultural Revolution" in China in November, 1965.

THE DYNAMICS OF SCHISM. World Communism may be characterized as a religious-ideological revolutionary movement. In this respect it can be compared with Christianity and Islam. True, Christianity and Islam are based on a belief in God as a point of departure, whereas Marx and his disciples were agnostic or atheist. But Confucius, too, was at least an agnostic, and the Buddhists were polytheists or atheists, depending on one's point of view. And the difference between believing in several gods, one god, or no god is less important for purposes of analyzing such movements than their similarities. The similarities are striking. Communism, Christianity and Islam have basic doctrinal principles, a complex set of behavioral strictures, an ultimate idyllic goal, all formulated in a body of scriptural literature. All three have prophets and martyrs. All have developed an institutionalized theocracy or atheocracy—church or party leadership—control of which is vigorously contested by individuals and groups.

Each of these revolutionary movements, particularly when young, convinced itself and its converts that it was unique and universal. These claims were exaggerated, and after a period of revolutionary expansion, they fell back on a series of accommodations with other faiths based on tolerance and a recognition of diversity.

More important in the study of the Sino-Soviet conflict is the dynamics of development inside these revolutionary movements. It is not hard to demonstrate that schisms have occurred, often bitter and debilitating.

There seems to be a schismatic tendency in religious-revolutionary movements. Certainly this is what happened in both Islam and Christendom.

After a spectacular burst of energy and unity during the life of Mohammed and immediately after his death, Islam endured the bloody schism between the Sh'is and the Sunes over issues so obscure that it takes a scholar to describe them. But they were so real to the people involved that into this century there continue to be periodic, bloody riots between the Sh'is and Sunes in such countries as Iran and Tanzania.

Christendom suffered one great schism, between Rome and Constantinople, in the fourth and fifth centuries, and then, in the sixteenth century an even more spectacular one, followed by religious wars both in England and on the Continent. Millions died in those wars. It is symbolic that it was only very recently, after nearly four centuries, that the Archbishop of Canterbury found the climate sufficiently ecumenical to pay a visit to the Vatican.

We are watching today an expression of this schismatic dynamic in the split between Moscow and Peking. And here the substantive issues are much more readily understandable than those which rent Islam, or those that separated Luther and Calvin from the Pope. In the Sino-Soviet rift, both protagonists have asserted their right to protect the purity of the faith from malicious or misinformed opportunists who threaten to distort and degrade it.

The same dynamic is pushing the Russians and the Chinese, as the two largest bodies in the fold of the Marxist believers, into a secular schism which will tend to follow patterns described above. Thus it will not make much difference whether the communes fail or succeed, whether Mao's pessimism on disarmament turns out to be justified or not. There is little chance that Moscow and Peking will reconcile their differences, yet it is unlikely that the Sino-Soviet conflict will escalate into a formal war. Though several thousand minor skirmishes did take place during the middle 1960s along the frontiers between Sinkiang and Kazakhstan, and particularly on the Amur, between Siberia and Manchuria, the Chinese are not apt to allow these incidents to build up into a war, particularly since the Russians have tactical nuclear weapons and the Chinese do not. Open societies sometimes lose control of local military circumstance and find themselves involved in wars no one wanted. Totalitarian states are less prone to this danger. It is significant that Japan and the Soviet Union became involved in a military conflict in 1939 at Khalkhagol, in Mongolia, involving armies in divisional strength, with artillery and air power, and thousands of casualties on both sides. Yet the conflict was well-screened from the rest of the world by censorship, and by mutual consent escalation was avoided.

The Sino-Soviet conflict will tend to go on even as future generations in both camps learn to question or even to doubt the infallibility, the "truth" of Marxism itself. For some religious and quasi-religious revolutionary movements persist and flourish even after doubt has replaced faith. And perhaps for this very reason. For doubt begets experimentation and progress, while faith often leads to complacency and stagnation.

To summarize: The Sino-Soviet conflict is serious and will last a long time. It will almost certainly lead to rupture, perhaps to military conflicts if not to all-out war. This animosity will be quite independent of the socio-political upheaval and intra-party power struggle now in progress in Mainland China, and also independent of the attitude and action of the West short of armed invasion of some part of the Communist bloc.

Finally, and for the U.S., most important: even if Asian intellectuals become embittered and disillusioned with the failure of the communes and the Great Leap (just as Western intellectuals were by the Russian purges of the 1930s and the Molotov-Ribbentrop pact), Communism, whatever its schismatic variants, will continue to have great drawing power, particularly in the world's underdeveloped countries, for a long time.

Recent works of Soviet writers and poets have been far more explicit and realistic than the declarations on China of Soviet political leaders. A poem by Andrei Voznesensky, published first in March, 1967, in Moscow and still without officially authorized English translation, is a good example. Voznesensky, perhaps Russia's greatest living poet, cries to the world to realize that Russia today again stands guard for the world against a new and frightful Chinese menace. A translation of this poem appears in Appendix III.

6. CHINA'S RELATIONS WITH OTHER COUNTRIES

MAO AND HIS colleagues have made strong efforts to create a favorable image in parts of the world that are not Russian. They have been taking special pains in their relations with the emerging nations of Asia, Africa and Latin America.

Communist China's conduct of foreign affairs has from the beginning been complicated by the continued existence of the Nationalist government of the Republic of China on Taiwan. The Peking government was early recognized by the entire Soviet bloc, as well as by India, Burma, Indonesia, Sweden, Finland, Holland, Denmark, Switzerland, and most of the Arab states. On the other hand, the U.S., Canada, Japan, the Philippines, Spain, Thailand, Malaya and most of the Latin American republics maintained relations with the Nationalists, who also retained China's place in the United Nations, including its valuable permanent seat on the Security Council.

The British, with characteristic flexibility, managed to keep a consul general in Taipei and a chargé d'affaires (but not an ambassador) in Peking. British recognition of Peking was based on a triple hope: first, that thereby London would be able to increase trade with Communist China; second, it would succeed in getting better information on developments there; and third, it might even influence the policies and attitudes of the Chinese Communists. None of these hopes materialized. The same fate befell Charles de Gaulle's similar aspiration when he recognized Peking in 1964.

From the very outset, the government in Peking has insisted that Taiwan is their internal affair and no concern of any other state. They have asserted that sooner or later they will liquidate the "bandit" government of Chiang Kai-shek, who, they claim, is able to maintain his position thanks only to U.S. "intervention." This position is based on the Cairo Declaration of 1943, wherein all the great powers agreed that Taiwan was a part of China. For Peking, the Nationalist government constitutes a threat to internal security, and also a major nuisance in the conduct of foreign affairs, particularly in areas where large numbers of Overseas Chinese reside.

Partly because of the incredible error of the Russians in walking out of a key meeting of the UN Security Council in June, 1951, that body passed a resolution to send troops to Korea, while earlier in February the UN General Assembly had adopted a U.S. resolution condemning Communist China as an aggressor. During more than two years of bitter warfare, Chinese "volunteer" forces fought South Korean, U.S. and other units under the UN flag. During this period the Peking government became understandably disenchanted with the UN and gave every evidence of having decided to follow its own policies in Korea and elsewhere, whether the UN or any of its members liked it or not.

But by the spring of 1952, the military and economic strain of the war had mounted, and the Chinese in effect sued for peace on a "before the war" status, and got it. Concurrently, Peking leadership no doubt decided on a more moderate posture in foreign affairs and proceeded to implement the decision in a series of conciliatory gestures toward India, Burma and Indonesia. In June, 1954, Chou En-lai went to Delhi to see Nehru. Their meetings culminated in the joint declaration of June 28, embodying the following five points of *Panch Shila,* to which the governments of Delhi and Peking pledged themselves:

1. Mutual respect for territorial sovereignty and integrity.

2. Non-aggression.

3. Non-interference in each other's internal affairs.

4. Equality and mutual benefit.

5. Peaceful coexistence.

Later the same year, Chou went to Burma and signed a similar agreement there. In his dealings with Indians and Burmese alike, Chou was cordial, conciliatory, friendly, and he so impressed Nehru that the Indian Prime Minister sponsored Chou at the Bandung Conference in the summer of 1955. There Chou pledged his government to the *Panch Shila* principles in its relations with all Asia and added two new points:

1. Recognition of the equality of all races.

2. Respect for the rights of all people to choose their own way of life as well as their own political and economic system.

This smiling new image was maintained in Geneva at the negotiations leading up to the end of the Indo-Chinese war and the partitioning of that country. And although the Peking government continued during the middle and late 1950s to give surreptitious material and moral support to Communist guerrillas in Malaya, South Vietnam and the Philippines, the period between the end of the Korean war and the first half of 1959 was characterized by an attempt to represent Chinese Communism as essentially peaceful, conciliatory and anxious to coexist at least with the rest of Asia in tolerant friendship. During this period China signed trade agreements with some ninety-four nations—bilateral pacts, for the most part, renewable annually—and traded vigorously with South and Southeast Asia, even trying on several occasions to establish serious economic relations with Japan.

The Tibetan rebellion set in motion expansionist tendencies among Peking's political leaders, which culminated in 1960 and later in a series of belligerent moves directed against India, Laos, South Vietnam, Thailand and even Indonesia. And the developments that followed did much to destroy the image of friendship.

In 1960-1962, the Chinese claimed and occupied some 50,000 square miles of what had previously been considered Indian territory, both in Ladakh and in the east, and pushed southward against Bhutan and Sikkim, whose weak governments were in no position to defend their territory against the incursions. These aggressive acts

93

against India lost the Chinese more prestige and influence. Nehru became bitterly anti-Chinese, as did many other influential Indians.

Witnessing this Chinese aggression against India, leaders of dozens of small new nations that otherwise might have been inclined to support Peking's claims for China's seat in the UN, withheld it. The Chinese withdrawal from northeast India did not improve their image because it so transparently reflected their military weakness rather than contriteness at their own aggression.

During the 1960s, Peking made major efforts to improve its relations with Australia, Canada and Japan. From the first two, China needed to purchase grain to feed its growing population. From Japan, and to a lesser degree from West Germany and the United Kingdom, the Chinese hoped to obtain chemical fertilizers and fertilizer plants, which they had finally recognized as being absolutely necessary for China to increase its food production. Peking was relatively successful in obtaining grain, purchasing roughly half a billion dollars worth annually during the mid-'60s from Australia and Canada, paying in hard currency earned largely from and through Hong Kong.

Preliminary trade negotiations with Japan were broken off in 1958 largely due to Peking's insistence on diplomatic recognition. They were resumed in 1962—without recognition—and a five-year trade agreement was signed under which Sino-Japanese trade increased substantially— to more than $600 million in 1966. This was only a small part of Japan's total foreign trade, however, and did not include Chinese coal or iron ore shipments to Japan, largely because of the poor quality and unreliability of delivery of these Chinese exports. It is believed that Chinese Communist prestige began to decline among Japanese intellectuals when in 1966 well-known figures such as Kuo Mo-jo, the intellectual leader, and Peng Chen, the mayor of Peking, were struck down by the "Cultural Revolution." The activities of the Red Guards and the general atmosphere in China were compared by many Japanese to that created by Japanese Fascism in the late 1930s. Nonetheless, the Japanese would undoubtedly like to expand trade with China, both for the sake of its economy and for its effect in improving relations between the two nations.

Though increasingly hostile to the United States in all of its public declarations, the Peking leaders nevertheless made major efforts to win friends here and in other English-speaking countries. In Peking a number of publications were printed in English and other Western languages—on good quality paper with quality photographs and art work. These were mailed at minimal cost to anyone who wished to subscribe in any part of the world. *Peking Review,* a weekly news magazine, and *China Reconstructs,* a monthly picture magazine about the same size as *Life,* are two among many. Radio Peking instituted an ambitious program of foreign language broadcasts. Indeed, a recent survey made by the British Broadcasting Company placed China third in the world in foreign language broadcasting with 732 hours a week, compared to 1,072 hours for the Soviet Union and 767 for the Voice of America.

Yet official relations between Peking and Washington have remained minimal and hostile. For more than a decade, periodic meetings have taken place in Geneva, then in Warsaw between the ambassadors of the U.S. and of Communist China. At these meetings routine issues have been raised and positions taken, including these: a) U.S. prisoners in China—at least a dozen at this writing; b) Chinese prisoners in the U.S.—allegedly hundreds, reportedly desiring to return to China but being frustrated by the U.S. government; and c) the exchange of news media correspondents which was discussed for years, but upon which no agreement has been reached. These Warsaw meetings were at least an official channel for communication between the two governments.

The present position of the Peking government is that it will have no further dealings with the U.S. and will permit no U.S. journalists to visit China as long as the U.S. continues its "aggression" against China by occupying Taiwan. The U.S. government position is that China stands condemned as an aggressor, and is therefore not acceptable as a member of the UN under its charter, and certainly not worthy of U.S. diplomatic recognition. Trade with Communist China is banned for all U.S. citizens or residents. But the fact is that these public positions are in both cases formal and might be changed at any time if such change seemed advantageous.

The question of UN membership for China is up to the UN General Assembly, which is now dominated by new nations in the developing world. At the General Assembly of December 6, 1966, a resolution to seat Communist China was defeated 57 to 46, with 17 abstentions. Worse from the Peking standpoint is that another resolution, declaring the issue of seating Communist China an "important question," thus requiring a two-thirds majority, was passed 66 to 48, with 7 abstentions. Even should some future General Assembly vote by a two-thirds majority to seat the Peking government, it would leave unsettled the legal question of the future of the Taiwan government—unless the Nationalists decided to cede their seat and permanent Security Council position to Peking, which is highly unlikely. Furthermore, Peking has stated that it would not accept membership in the UN as long as the "bandit" government of Taiwan is a member. Many observers feel that this impasse is likely to last a long time.

The Chinese government has gone to most extraordinary lengths to impress the peoples and the governments of new nations. Peking has been encouraged, by reports of unrest in many less-developed areas, to conclude that many developing countries are awaiting China's revolutionary guidance and assistance. The official China News Service recently reported "An excellent revolutionary situation prevails in Africa." It claimed that the thought of Mao Tse-tung was gradually being accepted as "the beacon light of the African revolution."

In the interest of impressing these new nations, the Chinese have engaged since 1954 in an impressive foreign aid program. Not counting military aid extended to North Korea since the Korean war and similar assistance to North Vietnam (which ran about $350 million in 1966 alone), Communist China has spent the equivalent of some $2.5 billion on aid programs to Communist bloc countries like Albania and feudal states like Yemen—and the whole range in between. Peking claims that in extending aid to less-developed countries, it "helps the recipient countries establish the necessary conditions to set up complete vertical industries—from raw materials to finished products." The experiences of these countries, however, indicate that Peking is long on words but short on deeds; being basically an agricultural country, China is not in a position to provide developing countries with modern industrial installations. Even small and medium projects promised to various nations have fallen far behind schedule.

Yet in 1966 alone, Peking pledged $28 million to Guinea and $2.8 million to Tanzania, as well as credits of undisclosed magnitude to Cambodia, North Vietnam, Nepal and Albania. In 1965, China gave $50 million in aid to Indonesia, $60 million to Pakistan, $28 million to Afghanistan and other loans and grants of unannounced size to Albania, Uganda and North Vietnam. The previous recipients of aid from the government in Peking included Kenya, Yemen (where a large group of Chinese workers is busy building port facilities), Congo-Brazzaville, Cuba, Ghana, Ceylon, Burma, the Mongolian People's Republic, Algeria, Syria, Somalia, and Hungary.

It is largely a result of this aid program that the Peking government has been able to offset hostilities created by its aggressive policies and to create a positive image in the minds of millions in Asia and Africa, and perhaps in Latin America. A thoughtful British diplomat, who served for years in Peking, summarized the elements in this image as follows:

1. The Chinese Communists eliminated foreign interference and reasserted China's national dignity.

2. They wiped out corruption.

3. They identified themselves with other "colored" people habitually humiliated by white Europeans.

4. They inspired fear of their military power.

5. They gained in stature by not talking about "freedom" and "democracy," which mean little in the underdeveloped world, but rather by emphasizing economic development through one's own efforts, which means much.

It is clear that this image has been tarnished or even destroyed in many areas by economic failures in China and by China's truculent attitude, particularly toward India. More recently, the convulsive spectacle of the Cultural Revolution undoubtedly has been costly to China's image around the world. In many countries of Africa and Latin America, Communist parties—long split into pro-Soviet and pro-Chinese factions—look with increasing favor upon the more responsible and moderate tactics of the U.S.S.R.

To summarize: During the past eighteen years, Peking's foreign policy has zig-zagged back and forth from broad smiles at Bandung to military invasion in Korea and India. The Chinese bid for leadership of the developing nations suffered severe setbacks in Africa in the early 1960s, in Indonesia in 1965 with the defeat of the Communist insurrection, and among Communist parties in many countries whose allegiances have swung toward Moscow's less belligerent line.

The Chinese have consistently attacked the United States as the devil image *par excellence*—perhaps only equalled in iniquity by the Soviet Union after the beginning of the Great Cultural Revolution.

The net result of Peking's conduct of foreign affairs has been the isolation of China from the Soviet bloc and the emerging nations, as well as from the capitalist states. At this writing, China's only friends are Pakistan, through the accident of common enmity toward India, and Albania.

7. CHINA'S ECONOMY IN THE MID-'60s

WHAT IS THE condition of China's economy at present? Any answer must begin with an analysis of the overriding fact of Chinese life: its population.

When the Communists won power over Mainland China in 1949, the population was thought to be about 450 million. The country's first scientific census, conducted in 1953, registered a population of 582.6 million—accepted by most demographers as realistic. Of this total, the census indicated that only 6 per cent, or some 35 million, were members of various national minority groups. The most important minority groups were the Chuang (6.6 million), Uighurs (3.7 million), Hui (3.6 million), Yi (3.3 million), Tibetans (2.8 million), Miao (2.5 million), and Manchu (2.4 million).

Since 1953, China's population has been growing, but no one is sure how fast. Another census was planned for 1963, but if it was ever taken, the results were not announced publicly, and most estimates of China's population today are based on projecting a 2 per cent or 2.2 per cent annual growth on the 1953 base. Such calculations would suggest a Chinese population of between 700 and 800 million in 1967.

Various factors may have kept the annual growth rate below 2 per cent. The first is birth control, a major government campaign that had been initiated in 1954. Simple contraceptive devices were made widely available in both rural and urban China, and legalized abortions and sterilization operations were performed free in hundreds of clinics. At the same time, early marriages were frowned upon by the Party, and often marriage licenses simply were not issued to "immature young lovers."

Attitudes changed during the Great Leap. Often quoted publicly was Chairman Mao's exhortation, "The people, and people alone, are the motive force in the making of world history." The implication was clear: China needed more people to build the country and to counteract the possible use of weapons of mass destruction by China's enemies. The birth control campaign was discontinued quietly in 1958 and not mentioned for four years, although clinical facilities were available for those desiring them.

Then, in 1962, the pendulum swung back again, and a major drive was begun to limit the country's population growth. Not only was marriage prohibited before the ages of twenty-eight for boys and twenty-five for girls, but far more repressive measures were used. Press reports from China in 1964 indicated that in many provinces a fourth child in any family was considered a "black" baby, not entitled to ration cards, and that the mother of such a child did not receive the usual fifty-six-day paid maternity leave. In 1966, reports from Kwangtung province told of obligatory abortions for mothers of two or more living children.

Other factors that may have curtailed China's population growth were the food shortages and the physical hardships of the Great Leap period, which probably reduced the number of live births and increased the incidence of early deaths.

Given these factors, many careful demographers in the U.S., Taiwan and India believe that China's population growth rate for the past decade has probably been below 2 per cent—perhaps 1.8 per cent—about the same as it is in the United States. Such a rate of increase would put China's 1969 population at just under 800 million, still an immense number of human beings who must eat to live.

It is interesting that the Chinese word for population, *jen kou*, literally means "human mouths," reflecting an ancient and realistic attitude of the Chinese toward their own large numbers. Possibly the Peking government will use further drastic measures to try to limit population growth to about 1 per cent a year, which is the Japanese rate. But this will be difficult to accomplish. Already there are more Chinese than can be adequately fed from the available lands at the present level of China's agricultural technology. Hence the sustained grain import program.

AGRICULTURE. The effective dissolution of the communes in 1960 and 1961 helped improve China's agricultural output. The private sector—the kitchen garden and the family sow and the chickens, which had always furnished a substantial part of China's agricultural production— again became operative. But even objective observers agree that the weather remained subnormal into the mid-60s in large parts of China and was a factor in keeping crops at a relatively low level.

Grain is the keystone of China's food economy, as it is in most countries. As pointed out earlier, the peak year in food grain production was 1958, when Peking first claimed 250 million tons, a figure later reduced and then simply forgotten. Experts in Hong Kong, however, estimate that crop at 193.5 million tons. Due to poor weather, however, to the diversion of agricultural labor to other efforts, to the shortage of fertilizers, and to the disarray of the Great Leap, subsequent production declined. It dipped sharply in 1959 and 1960, when it was 160 million tons. In subsequent years it regained some of the losses, then lost again. In 1966, the figure was at 175 million tons. For the yearly and comparative rates with the period prior to 1958, see Table VI in the Appendix.

China's food shortage was eased during the mid-60s by three factors. The first was the dissolution of the communes and the reinstitution of the kitchen gardens. The second was increased imports, about which more will be said. The third factor was that by 1965 China had paid the Russians both the interest and the principal due them under earlier aid agreements, and some $200 million worth of food products that had been exported annually to the Soviet Union during the early '60s was available for domestic consumption and for exports to other countries for hard currencies.

INDUSTRY. As we have seen, China's late-born industry made major progress during the first decade of Communist power. China had become an emerging industrial power by 1959 in every respect, except per capita indices of production or capacity, which were swamped by the country's huge population. Furthermore, China's huge coal reserves, probably the world's largest, and its considerable mineral resources were being exploited far more vigorously than even the most optimistic observers had considered possible a decade earlier.

Manufacturing industries made progress as indicated in detail in Table IV in the Appendix. Particularly impressive were the steep increases in production of coal, petroleum, steel, chemical fertilizers, locomotives and electric power. In both volume of production and in quality, China made great progress in two fields—military equipment and atomic installations. Actual production figures or estimates were not released, but taking industry as a whole, the best estimates of the experts in Hong Kong and Washington indicated that China will be lucky to achieve the 1960 targets—as stated in Table IV—in 1970.

For further details on China's current industries and the Chinese plans, product by product, Appendix II embodies the best information now available on the subject.

TRANSPORT. China's railroad network predated World War II; part of it even predated World War I. In 1966 it stood at 20,000 miles. Travelers say the passenger trains are clean and run on schedule. The road network is about 400,000 miles long, of which about 120,000 miles are paved. In 1966 some 300,000 trucks, 10,000 buses and 50,000 passenger cars were in operation. These facilities are inadequate for the needs of a country China's size. But they are supplemented by two of the world's longest navigable rivers and by an increasingly effective system of air transport operated by CAAC—China's national airline. By late 1966 this network was nearly 30,000 miles long, and included 50 air routes linking more than 70 cities. The national airline has about 500 planes, mostly IL 14s and IL 18s and Viscounts. A number of these planes are chronically inoperative for lack of spare parts.

China is linked by international airlines to Karachi via Pakistan International Airlines and to the Soviet Union via Aeroflot. There is no regular commercial air service to India or Japan; however, CAAC does operate some planes to Cambodia and North Vietnam.

China's sea-going merchant fleet consists of about 200 vessels with a total tonnage of approximately 1 million. Most of these ships were bought abroad and are old and relatively inefficient.

TRADE. Most of China's foreign trade during the 1950s was with the Soviet bloc. Indeed, three-quarters of China's peak of $5 billion worth of imports plus exports (in 1959) was carried on with the Soviet Union and its associates in Eastern Europe.

The Great Leap cut this total drastically as China failed to deliver because of internal strains and stresses. At the same time, growing hostility between China and the Soviet Union forced the Chinese to cut the proportion of their total trade with the Soviet bloc in order to avoid over-dependency on politically hostile governments. Thus in the 1960s, China's trade with Hong Kong, Japan, Canada, Australia and several West European countries increased rapidly, as Table V in the Appendix indicates.

In spite of the drain on Chinese resources caused by payments to the Soviet Union until 1965 for the "aid" received in the 1950s, and in spite of the U.S.'s virtual blockade of China which continues in 1967, China's role is becoming substantial in world trade, and its gold reserves have been built up to some $350 million above the level of 1960. For details on China's trade with non-Communist countries, see Table V in the Appendix.

Inside China, food products and consumer goods continued to be in short supply, and domestic trade was slowed by rationing of many items. But by 1965, the average Chinese was eating far better than he had during and immediately after the Great Leap, and foreign travelers reported that both rural and urban Chinese were reasonably well-dressed.

SCIENCE AND EDUCATION. Though China has made major efforts since 1949 in the field of education, these have largely been concentrated on elementary and vocational training. The country's research and advanced studies institutions have been staffed principally by Chinese trained abroad. For example, the director of China's Institute for Atomic Energy was trained in France and returned to China in 1948. One of his deputies was trained in Berlin, another in California, a third in Edinburgh, a fourth in St. Louis. Many of the second-ranking Chinese nuclear scientists were trained in the Soviet Center in Dubna, near Moscow, before the breakdown of the Educational Exchange program between the two countries in 1966. Most of China's top research and development scientists in fields from rocketry to mathematics to medicine and agriculture were trained outside China, and for the immediate future China does not have the educational facilities to train such specialists. This point was conceded in January, 1966, by the *People's Daily,* which stated that China would need twenty to thirty years to catch up with the industrialized nations in the West. The isolation from both the Soviet bloc and the West during the past several years will surely act as a further barrier to scientific development in China.

At the bottom levels, education in China has made considerable progress, in spite of enormous linguistic problems. The Chinese people speak many languages, different in vocabulary, different in grammar and different in structure. These languages are tied together for the literate by the written ideographs, which have no phonetic relation to the spoken words in any of China's languages. To read a serious book, one must know thousands of ideographs or characters; a Chinese typewriter is the size of a piano and requires a skilled operator; a Chinese dictionary is a tedious compilation. It requires page-by-page searching for an unfamiliar character that can be categorized only by the number of strokes needed to pen it. Thus no alphabet could replace the unwieldy ideographs for all China's languages, while to teach all Chinese to speak and read an alphabetized version of Kuo-yu or Mandarin would require at least a generation and could be expected to meet with regional objections from the hundreds of millions of Cantonese, Fukienese and other Chinese who would be forced to change languages.

Preoccupied with more pressing problems, the Peking government has undertaken no decisive language reform so far, and China's educational system at the elementary and secondary levels continues to suffer serious difficulties.

MILITARY FORCES. It is generally agreed that China's armed forces would be at an immense disadvantage in operations outside Chinese borders because of logistic and technological inferiority and particularly because of vulnerability to air attack.

For operations on its own soil, however, China's army is one of the world's best. Its 2.5 million men are organized into 150 divisions, of which about 130 can be regarded as combat divisions. The rest are transport, supply and auxiliary units. Of the combat divisions, about 100 are infantry, four are armored, three cavalry and three airborne. There are also two artillery divisions, largely distributed among the infantry divisions. Of the infantry divisions, two-thirds are light, the rest heavy. The former have no motorized transport and depend on manpower and pack animals for mobility. The latter have trucks and howitzers. All are well supplied with automatic weapons and mortars.

The Chinese army is now self-sufficient in all types of weapons and ammunition. Its disposition in 1967 is essentially defensive. The concentrations of divisions are in areas China feels might be attacked, not in departure points for foreign expeditions. The largest concentrations are in Manchuria and in the great plains between the Yellow and Yangtze rivers—the heartland reserve. About 600,000 men are stationed along the eastern coast, not more than 200,000 in the extreme south, along the borders of Vietnam, Laos and Burma. About a dozen divisions are around Peking, probably for security and political purposes.

China's air force has about 2,400 planes, almost 2,000 of them jets. Of these, 300 are IL 28s, 100 MiG 19s, 15 MiG 21s, 1,400 MiG 15s and 17s. China now makes spare parts for all these planes and may have been making its own MiG 19s as of late 1965. The country plans to make its own MiG 21s in 1967. The greatest concentration of air fields is in the northeast.

The Chinese navy is small and defensively designed and deployed. Only about 3 submarines a year are manufactured; about 35 are in operation. The navy has 40 destroyers and destroyer-escorts. The rest of the fleet consists of about 300 patrol and torpedo boats. Realizing the weakness of their navy, the Chinese so far have not committed any part of it to combat, even against the Nationalists.

China's total militia, or National Guard, is about 12 million strong. Only about 1 million of these are organized in combat-ready units. Most experts consider that the militia is of doubtful military value for domestic defensive purposes and of no value for any foreign operations.

NUCLEAR WEAPONS. For nearly all its eighteen-year-long life, Communist China has made substantial efforts in science, particularly in nuclear science. Some highly qualified Chinese have returned from top U.S. research institutions, and large nuclear research centers have been set up. The first reactor, obtained from the Russians in the mid-1950s, was installed near Peking. Later these efforts were concentrated in Lanchow and Paotow—which might be compared to the installations in Oak Ridge, Tennessee, and Hanford, Washington, though the Chinese installations are smaller and far less sophisticated. China's Alamogordo is at Lop Nor in the Gobi desert, where the Chinese detonated their nuclear devices in 1964 and 1965, and launched what they described as a "guided missile with a nuclear warhead" on October 27, 1966.

On June 17, 1967, less than three years after becoming a nuclear power, China announced that it had successfully exploded a hydrogen bomb. Detonated at Lob Nor, the bomb was estimated to have an explosive yield equivalent to 3 million tons of TNT.

Most experts agree that China will be unable in the foreseeable future to challenge either the U.S. or the U.S.S.R. in the quality, variety or quantity of nuclear weapons but that very soon the Chinese will have enough "bang" to do serious damage to near neighbors like the offshore islands of Quemoy and Matsu and Taiwan, and to frighten everyone badly.

GROSS NATIONAL PRODUCT. Over-all, China had in 1966 a Gross National Product estimated at about $70 billion, or about $100 per capita. This is nearly twice India's per capita level, but far below the level of other great powers. Japan's total GNP is about that of China's, though her population is about one-seventh the size. In 1965, Chinese agriculture accounted for about 4 per cent of the country's GNP, yet 80 per cent of China's population lives in rural areas.

The present per capita GNP is about that of 1957. Thus during the past decade, China—like Latin America— has been barely able to increase its total productive forces as rapidly as the population has increased.

This fact, coupled with the absolute decrease in the country's per capita food production, should give any Chinese leader or careful observer cause for serious concern.

8. THE REPUBLIC OF CHINA AND OTHER OVERSEAS CHINESE

THE NATIONALIST ARMIES, when they were defeated in 1949, fled to Taiwan. At that time this lovely island and the nearby Penghu, or Pescadores archipelago, had a population of 7.6 million Taiwanese-Chinese, who spoke the Fukien dialect. During the period of Communist takeover on the Mainland and for the next several years, nearly 2 million Mainlanders came to Taiwan. Generalissimo Chiang Kai-shek set up his capital in Taipei, whose population was then about half a million.

For half a century, the island had been under the colonial rule of the Japanese (they conquered the island in 1895). As they did in Korea, the Japanese had built schools and railroads and some industries, which were operated for the profit of Japan.

With their defeat in 1945, the Japanese withdrew, fulfilling wartime international resolutions to treat Taiwan as an integral part of China.

Some Taiwanese did not like the prospect of being governed by the Chinese Nationalists, whose corruption and inefficiency had been an important factor in their loss of the Mainland. The Taiwanese independence movement was crushed, however, and Chiang Kai-shek and his government proceeded to implement an impressive program to make Taiwan a showpiece for Asia, while awaiting the right moment to invade and recapture the Mainland.

One of their first economic measures was land reform. This was facilitated by the fact that the new authorities came from the outside. The Nationalist leaders owned no land on the island; indeed, some desirable land still belonged to the Japanese. This made possible an effective distribution of agricultural land to the farmers working it.

By late 1950, war damage on the island had been repaired, and the economy restored to its pre-war level. From then on, the Nationalists supervised a remarkable period of development, carrying out policies and maintaining standards of efficiency they had often failed to observe when they governed the Mainland.

The work was complicated by the large army they maintained—about 600,000 soldiers, sailors and airmen— poised to invade the coasts of Fukien across Formosa Strait. On the other hand, they received substantial economic and military aid from the United States with whom they had concluded a Mutual Defense and Assistance Pact. Total U.S. economic aid from 1950 through 1965 amounted to just under $1.5 billion, or about $100 million annually. Total military aid amounted to nearly $2 billion.

The economic aid program terminated in mid-1965. The military aid continues, and a large U.S. military mission remains on the island. The presence of these U.S. forces is constantly attacked by the Peking government which insists that any normalization of their relations with the U.S., or with the United Nations, must be preceded by the termination of "American aggression against China," the withdrawal of the "U.S. occupation forces from Taiwan."

The Taiwan government, which calls itself the Republic of China, stoutly maintains that it is the only legal government of China and will reassert its control of the Mainland as soon as possible.

The chances for a Nationalist invasion diminish year by year, as leadership ages and as the body of Nationalist troops becomes predominantly Taiwanese conscripts whose interest in retaking the Mainland is limited.

During the 1950s and early 1960s, Nationalist leaders like Chiang Ching-kuo, eldest son of the President, and Minister of Defense, insisted upon maintaining constant contact with a network of agents and a large body of secret supporters on the Mainland. They also claimed that the masses on the Mainland were ready to rebel, reporting numerous local "uprisings," which usually turned out to be attacks by hungry peasants on grain elevators, or on particularly unpopular Communist officials.

When civil strife did begin on a large scale during the Great Cultural Revolution, it was clear that neither the Maoists nor the Revisionists had any use for Chiang Kai-shek or his government. The Generalissimo had the objectivity and wisdom to recognize this. He and other Nationalist leaders realized that an invasion during the Cultural Revolution might drive the antagonists together again. Even if Chiang or some successor should decide to invade, the terms of the U.S.-Chinese pact forbid such action without American consent.

During both the Korean and the Vietnamese wars, many critics chided the Nationalists for failing to send part of their large and well-trained army to fight Communism there instead of talking about an invasion sometime in the future. The Nationalists responded that they were holding down up to forty divisions of the Chinese Red Army by their presence alone, which was a greater contribution than they could make in another theater. Besides, thoughtful leaders in Washington believed that a Nationalist Chinese expeditionary force in either Korea or Vietnam would cause more political trouble than it was worth. Only in the air, over the tiny but heavily fortified Nationalist islands of Quemoy and Matsu, did the Nationalists engage in actual battles in 1958. Here they did very well, shooting down thirty-six Communist planes while losing only six of their own, until the Reds broke off the engagement.

Perhaps more important than their military presence was the record of effective administration and economic development on Taiwan. During the fifteen years between 1950 and 1965, Taiwan's agricultural production doubled; its gross national product increased by an average of more than 7 per cent a year; its trade thrived; and many new industries prospered.

The average Taiwanese farm is only three acres, but two-thirds of the farms are farmer-owned. Diligence and the excellent extension services and technical assistance make possible an average of two crops a year. Taiwan has developed a number of new varieties of rice which have increased yields by threefold or more. The island produces sugar, soy beans, fruit, tea and mushrooms. Indeed, Taiwan stands first in the world in mushroom exports.

Due partly to the plentiful supply of food, the island's population increased rapidly. Births outnumbered deaths so heavily that the net annual population increase rate advanced to 3.6 per cent in 1963, one of the highest in the world. After that, a government-sponsored population planning campaign succeeded in reducing the rate to 2.7 per cent in 1966—still well above the world average.

The island's 600 miles of railroad and 10,000 miles of highways, its 1.5 million kilowatts of power production and its well-developed irrigation system give it one of the most developed economic structures in Asia.

Industrial production has been growing at an average rate of 13 per cent a year over the past decade. The country's finances are in good shape. The country's $188 per capita income in 1966 made Taiwan one of the most affluent nations in Asia.

Achievements in education have been outstanding. Free, compulsory attendance through the sixth grade is strictly enforced. In 1966, 2,189,000 pupils were in primary schools, nearly half a million in secondary schools, 111,000 in vocational schools and 64,000 in colleges and universities. This contrasts sharply with the situation on the Mainland where nearly the entire school system has been shut down by the Cultural Revolution.

Continued economic development in Taiwan will depend on foreign investment, because the island itself is woefully short of capital. Indeed, so scarce is money that savings accounts pay more than 10 per cent interest— one of the highest rates in the world. Government officials and foreign observers are confident that capital will be forthcoming in the years immediately ahead. They point out that in recent months a number of new electronic manufacturing enterprises have sprung up in Taiwan, thanks to investments from overseas.

Unfortunately, these impressive achievements in economic growth have not been matched by measures leading toward political democracy. Taiwan has but one political party. Neither opposition parties nor an opposition press is permitted. Generalissimo Chiang Kai-shek, as President, makes all important decisions, with advice and consultation from cabinet ministers whom he appoints and dismisses at his discretion. The legislature is virtually powerless.

What will happen when the "Gimo," now in good health, but nearing eighty, dies? Legally, the President will be succeeded at his death by Vice President C.K. Yen, who is ten years younger but in poor health. Competent observers believe, however, that Chiang Ching-kuo, fifty-seven, is likely to be very powerful after his father's death, whether or not he actually becomes President. As present Minister of Defense, head of the youth and veterans' organizations and very influential with the country's security and intelligence services, he already controls important sinews of power. Ching-kuo went to school in the Soviet Union in the 1920s when the Russians were helping the Kuomintang. He has a Russian wife, and speaks Russian grammatically, though haltingly because of lack of practice.

What is the future of Taiwan and its government? This depends, in great measure, on what happens on the Mainland. If the Communists in Peking succeed in stabilizing their control, then the pressure will be great on some successor of Chiang Kai-shek to make a deal. Indeed, periodically in Taiwan rumors are heard that Ching-kuo has been approached with an offer of a vice-presidency in the Peking government, life-long appointment as governor of the Province of Taiwan, and a marshal's star in Peking's PLA.

The rumors hold that he would have to agree to surrender Taiwan's seat in the United Nations and to allow the island to be integrated into China's economy and its political structure. Ching-kuo denies any contact with the Mainland, and indeed, he would be gullible to trust any commitments made by the Communists at this point.

On the other hand, if the present crisis in China leads to real civil war and fragmentation, then it is not impossible that some hard-pressed provincial governor along the coast might request assistance from Taiwan to help defend himself from punitive forces dispatched from Peking. In this case, both might swallow their pride and

112

bend their orthodoxy sufficiently to make possible an uneasy alliance under which the Nationalists might again find themselves on the Mainland.

Far more likely, however, is that the Government of the Republic of China will continue its present competent rule over Taiwan, whose people may eventually support rather than just acquiesce to this status. When that becomes evident, the conditions may be created for the evolution of a more democratic government in Taiwan.

Meantime, Chiang Kai-shek continues to enjoy UN membership, and his Government of the Republic of China is recognized by 57 nations and by most of the 15 million Overseas Chinese.

THE OVERSEAS CHINESE

In addition to the 12 million inhabitants of Taiwan, some 15 million other Chinese live in various parts of Asia, often in large unassimilated communities. Two large and prosperous cities—Hong Kong and Singapore—are almost entirely Chinese. There are large Chinese communities in Thailand—about 3 million; in Indonesia—about 3 million; in Malaya—some 2.5 million; in Vietnam—about 1 million, and smaller communities in Burma, Cambodia, the Philippine Republic and Japan. The Chinese in several large cities in the United States and Europe are gradually becoming assimilated, and in any case do not constitute independent and potentially important political and economic units, as do Overseas Chinese communities in Asia.

HONG KONG

This is a remarkable city. Its 3.8 million inhabitants are almost entirely Chinese. Most of them came to the British Crown Colony and its New Territories after 1949 as hungry, destitute refugees from the Mainland. Hong Kong had no agricultural base and little industry prior to that time but existed largely as a port and trading and financial center. It lacked enough water for its needs.

During the seventeen years after the Communist victory on the Mainland, Hong Kong became an important center for textile, electronics and chemical manufacturing as well as shipbuilding and repair. Huge blocks of office buildings were built, as well as prosperous suburbs on the islands and on the Peninsula of Kowloon. Massive complexes of houses were built where refugees can live in sanitary but modest housing for rents as low as three dollars a month. More than a million children are in schools. Medical care is among the best in Asia. Half a dozen large and ultramodern hotels handle half a million tourists a year.

Most of this construction is in the private sector and has been made thanks to about $200 million a year in foreign investments seeking security and profit in politically stable Hong Kong. These investments come from the U.S., Japan, and also from Overseas Chinese all over the world.

The city government, led by a few hundred competent British officials, has managed its economy so well that the efficient public services and utilities have been paid for out of income and from occasional land sales. Hong Kong has received no subsidy from Her Majesty's government in London and has borrowed nothing.

In 1967, a new catch basin was completed, freeing the city from the need to buy water from Mainland China except during periods of low rainfall. The continuing life of the city seems assured at least until 1997, when the New Territories lease runs out. By that time officials expect the city to have a population of 10 million.

Hong Kong is one of the most beautiful cities in the world. Its port teems with merchant vessels as well as with elements of British and U.S. fleets which come in for supplies, repairs or for rest and recreation of the crews. The Hong Kong airport, though a tricky one to get into because of adjacent mountains and the close proximity of Communist territory, is one of Asia's busiest. Some of Asia's most beautiful homes surround Repulse Bay. Hong Kong's many bays and channels furnish excellent yachting. Luxury yachts are anchored side by side with scruffy, patch-sailed Communist junks which sail into the harbor with loads of vegetables and fruit, and leave with fertilizer and petroleum products.

Why have the Communists so far tolerated this island of capitalist prosperity? The answer is, it pays.

Hong Kong buys nearly all its food from Mainland

114

China, and pays in the Hong Kong dollar—the Swiss franc of the Far East. But China buys little from Hong Kong, so that annually nearly half a billion dollars in much-needed foreign exchange goes to the Mainland from Hong Kong. In addition, the Chinese Communists use Hong Kong as headquarters for their international commercial and foreign operations. The large, gloomy Bank of China building in downtown Hong Kong blocks a corner of the view from the Governor's residence, and does a thriving business, not the least of which is handling remittances from Chinese all over the world. Some of these are simply gifts by Overseas Chinese to relatives on the Mainland. Some are funds sent as a sort of ransom, to guarantee relatives on the Mainland security from persecution.

Hong Kong is the principal channel of Communist Chinese exports, and has several large wholesale and retail stores where everything from motorcycles and sewing machines to fine jade carvings, wigs of the finest human hair, fancy tinned mushrooms and other delicacies can be purchased.

Hong Kong also abounds with Communist foodstores offering rice and other products for distant delivery. A Chinese might go to such a store and order a kilo of rice, worth, let us say, one dollar, for delivery to his aunt in Swatow. He pays a dollar for the rice, about a dollar for packing, shipping and insurance, and for "duty," about two dollars more. The rice goes directly from the Swatow paddy where it was grown to the consumer, and the Chinese Communists realize four dollars.

When all these forms of income are added up, Communist China earns well over half a billion dollars a year from and through Hong Kong. It is by far Peking's largest source of foreign exchange.

Periodically, the government in Peking makes a routine complaint about the continued occupation of Hong Kong by "British imperialists," but everyone knows that this is a formality. However, Communist-inspired riots in May, 1967, were serious. But as long as Hong Kong continues to be an important element in China's foreign trade and financial operations, it is unlikely that Peking will take any measures actually to evict the British, and the city will continue to be a neon-starred, glittering island of affluence and a haven for refugees.

SINGAPORE

Another excellent port, Singapore is located almost exactly on the Equator on the point of the Malayan Peninsula and within sight of the coast of Sumatra. Now an independent state, Singapore is governed by the People's Action Party headed by brilliant, British-educated and left-leaning Lee Kuan Yew. By Treaty, the British maintain a naval base in Singapore and several thousand ground troops, as well as their defense headquarters for East Asia.

Since the separation of Singapore from Malaysia, and particularly during the "confrontation" between Indonesia's President Sukarno and Malaysia, Singapore's port experienced a recession. Traditionally the export port for much of Indonesia's rubber and Malaysia's tin and rubber, Singapore suffered losses of revenue and some unemployment. But General Suharto's seizure of power in Indonesia following the Indonesian Communists' abortive coup of September 30, 1965, and his gradual removal of Sukarno from effective power in 1966, restored more normal business to Singapore.

INDONESIA

Indonesia's Chinese community of 3 million suffered drastically in the fall of 1965. During several nightmarish weeks, an estimated 500,000 "Communists" were murdered by Indonesian vigilantes or mobs. While thousands of Communists were killed and the Party's leadership wiped out, thousands of others were killed simply because they were Chinese.

In Indonesia, as in the Philippines and in Burma, the Chinese have developed ways of working together, and they have worked hard to give their children the best education available, even at great sacrifice. Over the years these Chinese have become more prosperous than their neighbors, which has led to jealousy and hostility toward them. Occasionally this animosity has burst out in "pogroms."

The Overseas Chinese in Asia have sometimes made

matters worse by treating others as inferiors by an implicit or explicit insistence that they are a "chosen people." This has been particularly true in Indonesia, where Chinese do everything they can to prevent their daughters from marrying Indonesians, and maintain—generation after generation—their own unassimilated communities.

This non-assimilation has been reinforced by the traditional attitude, accepted by both the Peking and the Taiwan governments, that a Chinese is always a Chinese—even after generations in another country, and even while serving in the armed forces of another state.

Only in Thailand (where the Chinese are mostly Fukienese, while elsewhere the Cantonese predominate) have the Chinese assimilated themselves into the indigenous community, indeed to such an extent that many government and business leaders in Bangkok, including several cabinet officers, are part Chinese.

In the rest of Asia, the Overseas Chinese remain unassimilated, living largely in urban communities. Though in most cases associated with the Nationalist government, if only because it offers them some consular protection, these Overseas Chinese could be a potential tool of Peking. And indeed, the Chinese did make up the bulk of the Communist terrorists in Malaya, whom the British fought and finally defeated.

Regardless of what happens in Mainland China, and even should there be fragmentation or a Nationalist restoration, the 15 or 16 million Overseas Chinese will continue to be a special problem in Southeast Asia. Their diligence, their clannishness—above all, their inborn and profound conviction of their own superiority—will hinder their assimilation into the social and economic life of the countries in which they live.

9. THE GREAT CULTURAL REVOLUTION

WHILE THE CHINESE economy gradually recovered from the disastrous Great Leap, subtler changes were taking place in the minds of many Chinese.

The peasants, now back in their own homes with their own kitchen gardens, their own sows and their own chickens, made it quite clear that they wanted to abolish the cooperatives entirely. This desire was shared by some regional party leaders. Both among the peasants themselves and among the local and regional leadership, complacency was replacing revolutionary fervor. Some local functionaries were slipping back into the age-old habits of petty graft and corruption characteristic of earlier regimes.

Factory workers in the cities began demanding higher wages, although production was not great enough to afford wage increases without sacrificing the investment program needed for new construction.

The thinking of professional soldiers was also changing as they studied the new equipment used in Vietnam and displayed in the maneuvers of many armies. They concluded that a military confrontation with the United States might be disastrous for China. They suggested two measures: first, a more moderate foreign policy calculated to reduce international tensions and make war less likely, and second, the re-establishment of friendly relations with the Soviet Union from whom China could hope to get modern arms. Both these measures were in direct conflict with Mao's advocacy of stepping up wars of national liberation to speed the victory of world Communism and concurrent vigorous struggle against Soviet revisionism.

In the cities, writers and other intellectuals were complaining of regimentation and censorship.

In the top party leadership, there were those who wanted to continue China's expensive foreign aid program, as opposed to those who would concentrate the country's attention on developing its own economy.

Finally, the revolution was getting middle-aged. The heroic zeal of the Long March was now only legend to the younger generation who found the puritanical austerity and frenzied work of the Great Leap silly, and looked for better paid jobs, more leisure, more enjoyment in life.

Travelers to China reported that prostitution, which had been almost wiped out during the 1950s, was again posing a problem for Communist officials. Hotel clerks, waiters and porters were accepting and even soliciting tips. The fanatical honesty that had characterized revolutionary China was being checkered by a resurgence of petty thievery. The compulsive cleanliness that had rid China of flies and kept its trains and public buildings immaculate for a decade was giving way to a more relaxed and comfortable traditional Chinese disorder. Businessmen from abroad remarked that it was becoming useful to silver a Chinese palm occasionally to facilitate a commercial transaction.

In short, China was still China.

Mao tried to arrest this back-sliding with the "socialist education" movement. In the countryside this campaign was sometimes known as the "Four Clean-Ups." Clean up politics, clean up thoughts, clean up organization, clean up economy. Essentially it was an ideological cleansing of the nation's 5 million intellectuals. Khrushchevian revisionism, Western capitalism and other ideas running counter to Mao's militant doctrines were suppressed. Countless "heretics"—philosophers, scientists, university professors, doctors, writers, and artists, as well as students—were ordered to the rural areas and barren hills to undergo an "ideological remolding" through manual labor.

"Never forget the class struggle," admonished Chairman Mao in September, 1962. "All erroneous ideas, all poisonous weeds, all freaks and monsters must be subjected to criticism without mercy."

Mao was dissatisfied with the results of the "socialist education" movement. He convinced the Party's Central Committee, meeting in September, 1965, that a purge was in order.

An all-out attack on the intellectuals appeared in *Wen Hui Pao*, a newspaper published in Shanghai. The paper attacked a book by Wu Han, entitled *Hai Jui Dismissed from Office*. This was the opening shot of the "Great Proletarian Cultural Revolution."

Written by Peking's Vice Mayor and Historian Wu Han, *Hai Jui Dismissed from Office* was a historical allegory ridiculing current political reality in Mainland China. It hinted sympathy and support of Marshal Peng Te-huai who had been dismissed by Chairman Mao from his Minister of National Defense post and replaced by Marshal Lin Piao in 1959. The reason for Marshal Peng's dismissal was that he had advocated a *detente* with the Soviet Union.

Professor Wu Han was the first of many victims. Next came Liao Mo-sha, another Peking intellectual, Teng To, a former editor of the *People's Daily*, and Peng Chen, Mayor of Peking and first secretary of the Party Committee in the capital. Peng Chen was summarily dismissed on June 3, 1966, on "anti-Party, anti-socialist" charges.

"Those who oppose Mao Tse-tung's thought," warned the *Liberation Army Daily* in its editorial on June 7, "at any time and no matter what kind of 'authorities' they are, will be denounced by the entire Party and the whole nation."

Students in all higher schools were urged to criticize professors and even deans and presidents who failed to toe the Maoist mark.

The purge spread. There was the dismissal of Lu Ting-yi, Minister of Culture, the Army Chief-of-Staff, General Lo Jui-ching, and President Lu Ping of the prestigious Peking University—to mention only several. All were denounced as members of a "black gang," who pursued a bourgeois and reactionary line.

To mobilize the mass base needed to carry out the Cultural Revolution, on June 13, 1966, the Central Committee of the CPC and the State Council announced a thorough reform of the higher educational system. Enrollment of new university students for the fall term of 1966-67 was postponed by six months (later extended to April, 1967). Under the new system, students would be admitted into a university not on academic merit alone, but on their knowledge of the thoughts of Mao Tse-tung. Sons and daughters of peasants and workers would be given higher priority for further studies than those of other classes in society. The criterion for acquiring a college education would no longer be academic achievement, but rather political reliability. "Better Red than Expert." Students who failed in their political reliability test would be "sent down" to the rural areas or labor reform camps, or assigned to the newly created part-work, part-study institutions.

Resistance against Mao Tse-tung persisted. Taking advantage of his absence from Peking between November, 1965, and early May, 1966, and again between mid-May and mid-July, 1966, a "handful" of top Central Committee members of the Party sent "work teams" to universities to restrict students' actions against academic authorities. When Chairman Mao returned to the capital from his retreat in Central China, during which period the seventy-two-year-old leader astounded the world by reportedly swimming for sixty-five minutes down the current of the great Yangtze River, he was furious that the "spontaneous actions" of the students against bourgeois and reactionary university authorities were being suppressed "from above." He convoked the eleventh plenary session of the Central Committee of the CPC in Peking from August 1 through 12. It was the first meeting of its kind in four years. Its final communique made no mention of the names of the Central Committee members and alternates who attended, but revealed that, unprecedently, representatives of revolutionary teachers and students of Peking were present. On August 8, the meeting announced its sixteen-point "decision."

A subsequent listing of the Central Committee membership showed that State President Liu Shao-chi was now downgraded from the generally accepted Number Two position to the Number Eight position in the hierarchy.

Lin Piao, the man behind the Communist gun, was proclaimed Mao's heir-apparent. *Red Flag,* the theoretical journal of the Party, declared that the sixteen-point decision was the "principal document and guideline" for the current cultural revolution. It added that the document was produced "under the personal supervision of Comrade Mao Tse-tung."

Clearly, Mao had defeated the opposition. Yet it must have been a shock to the old warrior and conspirator to realize that there had been so many of his old comrades to turn against him. If he was to succeed in provoking a new burst of revolutionary zeal and enthusiasm, a new nucleus of political power and mass base of support was essential.

The new power nucleus was the Cultural Revolutionary Committee, under the chairmanship of Chen Po-ta, Mao's former political secretary, and Chiang Ching, Mao's wife. The mass base was to come from China's youth.

After a careful survey of the huge Young Communist League, Mao apparently decided it was unreliable. He purged its fifty-two-year-old first secretary, Hu Yao-pang, for "revisionism" and proceeded to organize millions of young people into the Red Guards.

Mao closed all higher and secondary schools, and ordered millions of confused youths to form Red Guard units to carry out a new revolution.

The Red Guard movement was officially launched on August 18, 1966, during a "Rally of One Million" in Peking. At dawn, Tien An Men (Gate of Heavenly Peace) Square was officially described as "a sea of red flags," as Peking's masses and tens of thousands of Red Guards and students from various cities converged on the vast square. By year's end, seven other mass demonstrations had been held in the same location. According to official estimate, some 11 million "revolutionary" youths had taken part in the Red Guard rallies which served as a rare—perhaps final—chance for the youths to get a glimpse of the old and infirm "god-sun," Mao Tse-tung, who had turned seventy-three years of age on December 26, 1966.

At each rally, the participants brandished their red-covered copies of *Quotations of Chairman Mao* and loudly shouted, "Long Live Chairman Mao!" As the parade passed below the rostrum during the inaugural rally on August 18, scores of selected Red Guard youths rushed up to meet him. Mao wore an olive-green uniform of the People's Liberation Army—he had not appeared publicly in a uniform for ten years. He stood side by side, not with the Chief of State Liu Shao-chi, but with Comrade Lin Piao, Minister of National Defense.

Of course the Red Guards had not sprung into existence overnight. Their formation had been approved in a decision made during the eleventh plenum of the Communist Party's Central Committee. The Red Guards were composed of militant youths controlled by the Cultural Revolutionary Committee and backed by the army. Their objective was ". . . to struggle against and crush those persons in authority who are taking the capitalist road." Chairman Mao himself was the supreme commander of the Red Guards, while Comrade Lin Piao was the deputy commander.

"Revolution means rebellion, and there is rebellion in the soul of the thought of Mao Tse-tung," declared a wall newspaper posted by the Red Guards. "Daring to think, to speak out, to take action, to blaze the trail and to make revolution—in one word, daring to rise in insurrection—is the most basic and most valuable quality of a proletarian revolutionary." This declaration was a major guideline for the Red Guard vandalism and hooliganism that characterized the first public exploits of the vigilantes.

Two days after their official formation, hordes of teenagers from various middle schools and universities descended upon Peking's main streets to cause havoc and destruction. "We have declared war on the old world," they shouted, creating fear and terror among the populace. Historical old street names and shop signs were ripped down, replaced with new "revolutionary" names. Many homes were raided and personal possessions considered bourgeois, feudalistic or capitalistic were confiscated. Men and women were dragged out of their homes and beaten in the streets. Many suicides were reported.

One of the most disturbing events during the early Red Guard episodes was the sacking of the Peking Sacred Heart Convent, a Roman Catholic school operated by elderly European nuns. It spelled finis to the "freedom of

123

religious belief," which is formally guaranteed in the Constitution of the Chinese People's Republic. All the eight nuns of the convent were expelled from the country.

Another early victim of the Red Guard destructive orgy was the Central Institute of Arts in Peking where wooden figures of Buddha, the Goddess of Mercy and other valuable art objects were burned. Wrote the official New China News Agency in its August 25 domestic service: "In the afternoon of 24 August, a revolutionary fire was ignited in the Central Institution of Arts to destroy the sculptures of emperors, kings, generals, ministers, scholars and beauties, images of Buddha and niches for the Buddha sculptures. The revolutionary students and teachers of the institute said: 'What we have destroyed and crushed are not only a few sculptures, but the whole old world.' "

The Red Guard movement soon spread from the Chinese capital to other cities. In Shanghai vandalism broke out when militant youngsters destroyed traces of the "four olds"—old ideas, old culture, old customs and old habits. In prewar days, Shanghai was notorious as a "city of sin," and now a war was declared by the Red Guards against beatniks, flappers, foreign dolls, poker cards, Beatle haircuts. The Red Guard rampages in Canton, Nanking, Chungking and other major cities did produce opposition from local party headquarters and the public in North, Central and Southwest China. This incited the Red Guard units to a new frenzy.

In Harbin, the Red Guards decided to burn down the provincial CPC committee headquarters. Certain leading personnel of the local party committee were accused of suppressing the mass movement and undermining the Great Cultural Revolution. Clashes between Red Guards, on the one hand, and workers and party cadres, on the other, ensued in many provinces.

Then rival units of Red Guards formed in many cities. Fist fights broke out between local Guards and those sent down by the Red Guard headquarters in Peking. Soon at least three such headquarters appeared in Peking.

A disillusioned Red Guard who escaped to Hong Kong on Christmas Eve of 1966 told a news conference: "There is no organization and discipline whatsoever among the Red Guards. Several of us formed a group and set up headquarters. There are countless groups within the Red Guards with whatever queer names you can think of. I was the leader of a group called 'East Wind Red Guard Rebellion Corps' at Manchuli, a town on the Chinese side of the Chinese-Russian border." Later the nineteen-year-old student was ordered to Canton in South China to take part in a "long march" which would eventually take him to Yenan. He told his story in clear, matter-of-fact terms: "We played the bully, beat up people and raised hell everywhere we went, and nobody dared to stop us because we were doing everything in the name of revolution. We were moving like locusts. We did not pay for what we ate and took away. If we thought that a place was nice and the food good, we would stay for a few more days. If not, we would stay overnight or just keep on going. Some of us felt ashamed of what we were doing, but we could not help it. We had to follow the trend."

Events were not conforming to Mao's anticipations when he and Lin Piao launched their "storm troop" tactics to rout out the enemy. Party officials and army officers were mustering their own followers among the peasants and workers and setting up Red Guard units of their own in various localities to oppose the "Peking" Red Guards. In part, this anti-Maoism reflected the regionalism latent in China. It was helped by the fact that in many of China's provinces the same man had acted as governor and army chief for a number of years and had begun to identify his province with his own ambition. For example, one of the provincial leaders who successfully repelled Peking Red Guards was Wang En-mao, the party chief in Sinkiang and also commander of the Sinkiang military region. Indeed, not only did Wang En-mao resist the Red Guards, but he also dispatched a division of his troops toward Peking for a showdown. This threat of civil war was avoided by a compromise. But others were to arise.

In a joint editorial on New Year's Day, the *People's Daily* and *Red Flag* asserted that the Cultural Revolution would be intensified in the coming year. Drawing a clear line for the course of the revolution, the joint editorial said:

"Nineteen-Sixty-Seven will be a year of all-round development of class struggle throughout China.

125

"It will be a year in which the proletariat . . . will launch a general attack on the handful of persons within the Party who are in authority and are taking the capitalist road, and on monsters and demons anywhere in society."

Meanwhile, foreign correspondents and Peking wall posters reported clashes between Red Guards and local workers and peasants in many areas in East, Central and West China. Japanese newsmen based in Peking reported on January 6, 1967, that fifty people were killed and nine hundred injured during serious riots between pro-Mao and anti-Mao elements in Kiangsu province. The Soviet Party newspaper *Pravda* reported January 8 that several thousand local workers clashed with Red Guards in Anhwei province. In Szechuan, according to the same paper, the Southwestern Bureau of the Chinese Communist Party and the Szechuan Provincial Committee came under Red Guard attack.

Judging by the mounting widespread opposition against Mao and Lin, many observers surmised that the Mao elements were in the minority. Chiang Ching, wife of Chairman Mao, hinted as much during one of her speeches. She said that numbers do not mean a thing; what counts is that one must have the correct class viewpoint by grasping the truth of Marxism-Leninism and of Mao Tse-tung's thought. Reading between the lines, China-watchers in Hong Kong and elsewhere deduced that the "handful" of those in power and taking the capitalist road were in reality a majority.

As month followed month and the Red Guard continued its destructive activities from one end of China to the other, an astonished world looked on in disbelief. All schools were closed in a country always most solicitous of education. The Red Guards burned bourgeois books and furniture. They blockaded the Soviet Embassy in Peking for weeks. They prevented the departure of international airliners. They invaded factories and offices, disrupting production. They stopped trains. They fought with workers; they fought the army; they fought among themselves. In Peking alone three separate and competitive "commands" of Guards vied with each other for power.

Periodically Chairman Mao appeared in public and nodded his approval. Chou En-lai and his Foreign Minister, Chen Yi, who at the beginning had seemed skeptical about the Great Cultural Revolution, supported the movement, but they cautioned against "excesses," publicly chiding the Guards for beating to death the Minister of the coal industry, in February, 1967.

Finally, in late February, Mao called a halt. The schools were ordered reopened, and the millions of youths were told to go back to their studies.

The Cultural Revolution went on, nevertheless. Now, the army took it over. An editorial in *Liberation Army Daily* stated: "We (the People's Liberation Army) must follow Chairman Mao's teachings and support the proletarian revolution. . . ." In Fukien province, the army took control of industry and government without serious resistance. But thousands were killed as workers and peasants fought the army. The Maoists claimed that they had seized power in Shanghai, Shansi, Kweichow, Heilungkiang and Shantung, as well as Peking itself.

In the rest of the country, officials who had been appointed by Liu Shao-chi and presumably were loyal to him remained in power. Liu himself was thought to be under house arrest in Peking as the leader of the revisionists.

The army was divided, some units having participated in Maoist take-overs under the orders of Lin Piao. Other units, Peking complained, were misled into supporting the revisionists who in many provinces had sought to assure themselves local support by granting workers' wage demands and promising peasants that there would be no return to the commune system.

In distant Sinkiang and Tibet, as well as in Inner Mongolia and in the northeast, fragmentation threatened as local governors and military leaders defied Peking.

The Party as such had ceased to be in control of China. Power was divided. The army held part of it; the Cultural Revolutionary Committee held part of it; and also holding part of the power were the local organs, assorted local leaders of the Committee, and, of course, the revisionists.

The economic effects of the Cultural Revolution could

127

not immediately be evaluated. The 1967 crop prospects were poor. Then to Hong Kong came ominous reports of disease epidemics in South China. A convulsed China tottered on the brink of fragmentation and anarchy.

10. THE FUTURE OF CHINA

CHINA IS CURRENTLY threatened with political fragmentation and economic breakdown. A consideration of its future by the nature of things must start with several different hypotheses.

1. The Maoists may win the current struggle and re-establish control over the Party and the country, or

2. The "revisionists" may win, or

3. A compromise may be reached and a type of coalition or collective leadership may emerge to try to run the country, or

4. The country may split into competing units, as has happened so often in Chinese history, particularly in periods of dynastic change, or

5. The Nationalists may make use of chaos and fragmentation in China to invade the Mainland and re-establish their power. Finally,

6. China may get involved in a major war with the U.S., as with the U.S.S.R.

Let us examine these contingencies in order:

1. Let us assume Mao wins. He is pledged to continue the aggressive foreign and domestic policies that have brought China to its present international isolation—its rupture with the Soviet Union and its explosive internal tensions. Mao has made clear his formula for dealing with these problems; at home, a new Great Leap, another convulsive effort to find a shortcut to Communism through frantic mass action and centralized totalitarian leadership;

abroad, relentless struggle against American imperialism and its reactionary running dogs, including the Soviet revisionists. Mao is further committed to the industrialization of China, and priorities can be expected to continue to starve agriculture of investment capital and top leadership. Finally, Mao is pledged to impose on China's intellectuals and young people political aims and procedures symbolized by the slogan "Better Red than Expert."

In this event, it is unlikely that Mao would intervene actively in the war in Vietnam or in military hostilities with either the Soviet Union or India. Mao is not squeamish about violence, but until he has an effective nuclear weapons system, he is vulnerable to devastating attack by either the U.S. or the U.S.S.R. or, as the Maoist propagandists suggest, both. Mao's attitude to the United Nations might be expected to remain intransigent as outlined by Chou En-lai: "The UN is by no means sacred or inviolable. We can live very well without it. . . . If the UN cannot be made to serve the interests and aspirations of the emerging nations, then another UN—a revolutionary UN—may be created in competition with that body which calls itself the United Nations but is in reality a tool of U.S. imperialism and therefore can only make mischief and nothing good."

Mao could be expected to continue to oppose nuclear test ban and arms control agreements as "anti-Chinese" machinations of the Soviet-American imperialist coalition, and to insist that "only a victorious socialist revolution all over the world can assure peace and a world without arms."

Mao's international strategy, pending perfection of his nuclear weapons, would be to support revolutionary and national liberation wars wherever possible, to continue currying favor in the eyes of the emerging nations and their governments with an economic aid program and to encourage the Vietnamese war, all the while seeking to hasten the day when the U.S., the European nations and the Soviet Union will be surrounded and engulfed by the emerging forces of the world—very much as he was able to surround and finally to engulf China's Kuomintang-held cities with his Communist-led peasant masses.

If Mao should happen to win the current conflict within

China, his pursuit of these policies, domestic and foreign, is likely to produce chaos and fragmentation and perhaps counter-revolution within a few years. Mao has already alienated millions of Chinese, including the young people on whom he has counted so heavily. A Red Guard who defected to Hong Kong in January declared: "Most of the Guards in my unit were really anti-Mao. But there didn't seem any immediate alternative to following orders. . . ."

The peasants are fearful of a new commune movement. The intellectuals are thoroughly disgusted at seeing professors marched through the streets in dunce caps and painted faces, being spat upon because they could not recite the thoughts of Chairman Mao. The workers want more wages. Many top Party leaders, as well as millions of other citizens, realize that Mao has made two grave errors: he placed far higher priorities on industry than on agriculture, and he sought to impose China's power on Asia and the world beyond its capacity and in disregard of the realities of world power ratios.

This leads to hypothesis number two:

2. On the basis of all these considerations, it is far more likely that the revisionists will win the struggle for power inside China. In this event, prognostications are more difficult, because the revisionists are not a clearly defined or structured political force. Their leaders must be presumed to be Communists, but they are Communists who have learned from the mistakes of the past decade and are anxious to diminish world tensions, to patch up conflicts with the Soviet Union, and to develop a more relaxed economic pattern at home, with less regimentation and more freedom of thought and movement.

If new leaders with these convictions do come to power, they could make an impressive impact on world events. By simply withholding support to Hanoi and refraining from goading the Viet Cong into continued sacrifices, they could be instrumental in bringing about a cease-fire there within days or weeks. By contributing to a Vietnamese cease-fire, the Chinese government would stand to save itself the nearly half-billion dollars a year it is spending on food and supplies for Vietnam and on some 50,000 Chinese road and bridge repair crews now at work in that country. Such an action by China would predispose many

131

nations to vote Mainland China into the United Nations, and if at that point the new government in Peking agreed to an independent Taiwan, world tensions would decrease substantially. China might even obtain substantial economic aid to help fill its need for investment capital for industrialization and modernization of agriculture.

Such a Chinese government would probably be unable to establish sincere friendly relations with the Soviet Union. The issues separating the two countries are too deep and irreconcilable for that, but an improvement in relations could certainly be achieved.

China would still want to reassert its influence over countries which it once dominated, such as Vietnam, Malaya, eastern Siberia and Soviet Central Asia, but it might well have the wisdom to show restraint. The government would presumably seek to perfect a nuclear weapons system, but would probably give to this effort and to foreign aid and heavy industrialization a far lower priority than at present. It would also step up radically its attention to the fertilizer industry and to agriculture. If such a China did perfect nuclear weapons, it would probably be inclined to use them to strengthen China's voice in world affairs. And it would probably use the weapons as a deterent force, particularly in Asia, rather than for aggression.

3. Hypothesis number three assumes that the internal conflict in China will end in a compromise, or a coalition, and if this comes to pass, all that need be said is that the Chinese will follow policies somewhere between the two alternatives just described.

So far we have considered three contingencies. Should any one of them materialize, China will face a monumental, nearly insoluble problem: to feed 800 million people in a country whose land will not support that large a population at its present level of technology. Already China must spend most of its available foreign exchange for grain. Today, 30 per cent of the food eaten in China's coastal cities comes from Australia and Canada. Hunger haunts whole provinces, and serious epidemics of meningitis and encephalitis have been reported. Peasants in several provinces are reported to have seized grain reserves and to have refused to make rice deliveries to the government.

Some Western theorists have suggested that China is on the verge of an economic take-off such as that which took Japan within a few years from late feudalism to its highly industrialized and prosperous present state, in spite of having lost a disastrous war. Although intriguing to contemplate, it seems highly unlikely that China can accomplish the same feat now.

Japan's take-off followed the Meiji restoration of 1868. It really got going only after Japan decreed free compulsory primary education in 1882, the surge being facilitated by the country's racial and linguistic homogeneity, its island security from attack, and the diligence of the Japanese people. And then, it took three generations for the surge to turn the tide in favor of Japan's consumers.

Of all these, diligence is the only one working for the Chinese. China's rural masses are still largely illiterate. The country is anything but homogeneous. It does not have insular security from attack. And China does not have three generations. China's crisis is now.

A more instructive analogy than Japan is Taiwan. In 1945, the island was on an economic par with Mainland China today. Then, in 1950, after war damage was repaired and an effective land reform launched, economic take-off began. The results were impressive. Ranking after Japan, Taiwan boasts the best developed infra-structure in Asia. The people are well-fed and clothed, industry generates enough capital to sustain boisterous growth. But what did this cost in outside investment? The United States furnished the development and seed capital as economic aid, which amounted to about $1.5 billion, or about $100 million a year between 1950 and 1965 when the aid ended, for an island whose average population for the period was about 10 million—or $10 U.S. per capita per year. If the capital-output ratio achieved on the Mainland were comparable to that of Taiwan during its take-off period, Mainland China would require $7 billion a year for fifteen years. This is more than twice the total of U.S. annual aid to all nations. It is more than total world aid. There isn't that much money available for economic aid, even if China somehow contrived to get the entire pot.

133

Even if the government of China managed to bring population growth rate down to zero—by such measures as issuing no ration cards to third babies and refusing women their free maternity leave after two living children —China would still face mass starvation in the next several years.

4. We come to the fourth contingency: fragmentation and economic chaos. If this occurs, as it so often has, China's population may be drastically reduced by epidemics and civil war. The long-term results are unclear. Possibly the Russians would contrive a kind of protectorate over Singkiang, Inner Mongolia and Manchuria— all areas bordering on the Soviet Union—and among China's richest in mineral resources. India, which already has a Dalai Lama, might well attempt some similar arrangement with Tibet. All this would leave China's basic problem unsolved because three of these provinces are sparsely populated.

Should Russia and India take over these areas, the identity and political beliefs of the regional leaders who emerge would have a profound effect on future developments. It is impossible to speculate on this matter. It might only be said that the Communist Party, although embattled and divided, remains at this time the only serious reservoir of power in China, with the possible exception of the People's Liberation Army. Local leaders would probably come from one of these two organizations.

It is interesting to know that thoughtful Russians are apprehensive of an unpredictable "Nasser" type leader emerging on top in the event of civil war and fragmentation in China.

5. Our fifth contingency is a Nationalist reconquest of the Mainland, probably in the wake of civil conflict and perhaps fragmentation or war. This contingency is extremely unlikely. For no evidence from the Mainland gives indication of any inclination on the part of any group there to invite the Nationalists back.

A Nationalist reconquest would be an economic disaster for the United States. For in this event, we would be obligated, not only morally but by treaty, to feed China and to help solve its other problems.

134

6. Our final contingency is a major war. This is unlikely. Should it occur, China would be most vulnerable to air attack and blockade, and the Chinese could take no comfort in the hope of carrying out offensive operations on any scale in retaliation.

No matter what happens, the Chinese are in serious trouble. Like a man grossly overweight, China's health and its importance in the world are not dependent on or proportionate to its mass.

Other large countries, indeed whole civilizations have fallen and disappeared as a result of poor leadership and misfortune. Such a fate may lie in store for China. United States experts feel that the best that can be done by whoever leads China is to give top priorities to agriculture, to give the peasants a freer hand and to introduce incentives in both agriculture and industry, while relaxing international tensions and hostilities, so that other countries will be encouraged to extend long-range economic aid.

What policies might the U.S. most appropriately follow in dealing with China during this difficult period?

In the first place, let us accept the fact that the government of China under Mao Tse-tung is bitterly hostile, desperately motivated to fight its way out of what it feels to be isolation and encirclement. Sensing this fact, our military strategists are constantly studying the possible variant of "taking out"—of physically destroying—China's nuclear weapons research facilities before the Chinese disperse them or bury them so deeply that such a step would no longer be possible. Even laymen know that China's nuclear facilities center around Lanchow, Paotow and Lop Nor, corresponding roughly to Oak Ridge, Hanford, Washington and Alamogordo in this country. These are sparsely populated areas, and civilian casualties would be minimal in the event of such a pre-emptive strike.

The decision to undertake such an action might follow subtle consultations with the Russians who have their own reasons to deplore China's emergence as a full-fledged nuclear power.

With reference to United Nations policy, we would be well advised to halt our attempts to prevent the General Assembly—a body constantly growing and increasingly dominated by new nations in the developing world—from inviting Peking to take a seat in the UN. If Peking declines, then the position of the UN would be strengthened and China will have further isolated itself.

In view of the treaty relations between the U.S. and the government of the Republic of China in Taiwan—and the importance of that government as a representative of the Overseas Chinese—it would seem unwise for the U.S. to extend formal diplomatic recognition to Peking until and unless the two Chinas somehow contrive to establish relations with one another. At the same time, we most certainly should discontinue our repeated assertions that the government in Taiwan is the government of all China, since for nearly two decades it hasn't been.

It is most important that the U.S. reestablish a dialogue with Mainland China. The hardening hostility of the Soviet Union to us is evident in its massive support of the Vietcong and North Vietnamese, in its intervention in the Middle East and in its suppression of pro-Western tendencies in Eastern Europe and even in the Soviet Union itself. These developments create a climate in which we should logically use the most elementary tool of power politics and diplomacy, the triangulation of forces—the use by A of B against C in the interests of A. But because we have no effective dialogue with China, we are deprived of this possibility. Nor would diplomatic relations with Peking be necessary to rectify this unfortunate situation. The resumption of the ambassador-level periodic Warsaw talks between China and the U.S., and the signature of *Panch Shila* by the two parties—measures suggested by Peking in December, 1968—would be a good beginning. If, further, we relaxed our embargo on trade with China, which is ineffective in any case, and established some pattern of cultural, scientific and educational exchanges, we would exert restraining pressures on the Russians and vastly increase the flexibility of our own position.

Such actions on the part of the new administration in Washington would not meet with much organized resistance in the U.S. The "China Lobby," a group of powerful Chinese and Americans with private and political interests in China, which is supposed to have exercised so much influence over U.S.-China policy, passed into limbo with the deaths of Alfred Kohlberg, Senators McCarran, McCarthy and Bridges, and with the retirement from politics and from the headlines of Senators Knowland and Jenner. The fact that General Wedemeyer, Admiral Radford and the State Department's Walter Robertson are out of the news, too, has helped to seal the tomb of the lobby.

That China has been exploited by Western white men in the nineteenth and twentieth centuries is well accepted. That the Chinese people have felt provoked into a backlash of hatred against the U.S. is as obvious as the Communists' self interest in using this sentiment for their own purposes. It is clear that for the Peking government, the U.S. is by definition the leader and the symbol of Western imperialists. Thousands of Americans were killed in Korea by Chinese bullets, and inestimable is the number of Chinese killed on many sides by American weapons, if not actually fired upon by Americans. Millions of Chinese are told daily that the U.S. is their worst enemy, and they have little other information upon which to base a judgment.

But observations and surveys in countries such as the Soviet Union, where the U.S. was also villified for years, show that the people often did not believe what they were told. It is possible that millions of Chinese similarly have immunized themselves from brainwashing and remain tolerant and friendly, as is the Chinese characteristic, aware of and grateful for the American assistance their country received over the past century in education, medicine, and economic aid of many kinds.

The current convulsions in China will probably end somehow within the next several years, leaving most Chinese feeling that the Communists may have been good organizers and may have contributed to a stronger and more dignified China, but that over two decades their mistakes outweighed their contributions. Communist ideology is not in harmony with the "heaven" that for millions of agnostic but essentially religious Chinese symbolizes God.

United States policy must in the end be directed toward establishing contact with and re-establishing the confidence of these Chinese. The revisionist Communists appear to be the most likely vehicle for the realization of this objective.

We shall do well to remember that China, though huge, is currently weak and corroded from within. It is a hungry dragon, misled by illusions, whipped to hysteria by external enemies and inner doubts and fears. A superannuated nation, its population pressures alone make it a danger to itself and to its neighbors, a danger the more real because its brilliant and diligent people have immense potential for good and for evil.

APPENDIX I

TABLE I

Leading Chinese Communist Commodity Exports to the USSR, 1959-1965*
(VALUE IN 1,000 RUBLES; 1 RUBLE = 1.1 U.S. DOLLAR)

Commodity	1959	1960	1961	1962	1963	1964	1965
Rice	74,316	49,666	286	18,351			
Clothing & household linen	173,849	173,814	157,739	162,953	143,514	107,311	49,071
Textiles, woven	139,968	125,569	113,705	106,523	87,395	41,379	24,120
Textiles, fibres	82,535	58,752	24,575	12,481	7,727	6,042	3,214
Vegetable oils, edible	18,915	8,383					
Meat & dairy products	41,840	17,584	1,702	5	2,328	22,289	55,142
Leather footwear	33,037	37,592	12,705	13,182	6,484	4,773	3,525
Metal ores & concentrates	65,977	55,057	43,459	31,813	23,299	11,909	not listed
Vegetables, fruits, berries & produce	—	16,416	8,671	11,664	13,002	16,874	11,307

TABLE I (cont'd)

Leading Chinese Communist Imports from the USSR, 1959-1965*

Commodity	1959	1960	1961	1962	1963	1964	1965
Complete plants	359,785	336,459	71,018	7,960	13,113	11,186	3,513
Power equipment	16,792	13,096	5,897	747	257	329	533
Railroad rolling stock	67,861	4,889	317		42	41	12
Automobile transportation & garage equipment	30,805	40,416	5,902	9,089	10,373	8,875	17,031
Oil-well drilling equipment	6,774	5,599	620	2	102	679	777
Metal cutting machine tools	5,951	3,022	870	61	232	382	4,790
Tractors & farm machinery	6,978	8,192	1,630	1,404	6,788	6,397	11,561
Excavators & road-building equipment	3,616	5,064	419	2	298	494	6,110
Petroleum products	94,395	90,871	108,599	72,469	54,666	19,422	2,005
Ferrous rolled stock	26,450	33,427	16,645	15,031	15,036	12,984	22,086
Non-ferrous rolled stock	3,115	4,891	2,257	1,798	1,350	706	627
Pipes	12,961	12,260	7,728	6,213	6,501	3,641	5,909

*Source: *Vneshnaya Torgovlya* (USSR Foreign Trade Statistical Book).

TABLE II

Year	Mainland China World Trade (in U.S. $ million)	Sino-USSR Trade (in U.S. $ million)	Percentage*
1959	4,182	2,055	49%
1960	3,866	1,665	43%
1961	2,899	919	31%
1962	2,739	750	27%
1963	2,785	600	22%
1964	3,255	450	14%
1965	3,800	417	11%
1966	4,100	350	9%

*SOURCE: Economic analysis by qualified experts in Hong Kong, January, 1967.

TABLE III

Communist China's Trade Aggregate with the USSR*
(VALUE IN 1,000 RUBLES; 1 RUBLE = 1.1 U.S. DOLLAR)

	1959	1960	1961	1962	1963	1964	1965
China's Imports	859,011	735,400	330,600	210,100	168,500	121,800	172,500
China's Exports	990,300	763,300	496,300	464,700	371,700	282,800	203,000
Total:	1,849,311	1,498,700	826,900	674,800	540,200	404,600	375,500

*SOURCE: *Vneshnaya Torgovlya* (USSR Foreign Trade Statistical Book), 1966.

TABLE IV

Mainland China's Industrial Production of Selected Items

	Coal 1,000 tons	Electric Power (million KWH)	Petro-leum (1,000 tons)	Steel (1,000 tons)	Cement (1,000 tons)	Chemical Fertilizer (1,000 tons)	Textiles (million cubic meters)	Trucks (by unit)
1949	32,430	4,308	121	158	661	27	1,890	Not published
1952	66,490	7,261	436	1,349	2,861	181	3,830	Not published
1955	98,300	12,278	966	2,853	4,503	332	4,360	Not published
1957	130,000	19,300	1,460	5,350	6,860	800	5,000	7,500
1958	270,000	27,530	2,264	8,000	9,300	1,240	5,700	16,000
1960	335,000	55,500	4,500	18,450	13,500	2,480	7,600	29,000
1962	190,000–	30,000	5,300	7,000–	6,000	2,120	3,000–	3,000–
	200,000			8,000			3,300	5,000
1963	210,000	31,000	5,900	7,000–	7,000	2,800–	3,300–	10,000–
				8,000		3,000	3,600	15,000
1964	220,000	32,000	6,000–	8,000–	8,000	3,400–	4,000–	20,000–
			7,000	10,000		3,600	4,500	25,000
1965	240,000	46,000	9,000	11,500	11,500	4,500	5,500	30,000

NOTE: The figures above for 1949-1958 are those published by Peking and are considered plausible by Western experts.
The figures for 1962 are Peking's published targets.
The figures for 1962-1965 are estimates by Hong Kong experts. During these years Peking published neither claims nor targets.

TABLE V

China's Trade with Non-Communist Countries
(VALUE IN MILLION U.S. DOLLARS; SELECTED COUNTRIES ONLY)

COUNTRY	CHINA'S IMPORTS					CHINA'S EXPORTS				
	1962	1963	1964	1965	1966	1962	1963	1964	1965	1966
West Germany	31.1	15.40	24.47	78.96	128.8	93.3	40.84	51.74	72.70	92.4
United Kingdom	24.1	37.40	49.96	72.34	89.48	64.8	51.88	68.96	83.22	94.81
France	43.3	58.39	49.61	60.09		16.9	21.09	30.84	43.70	
Italy	19.0	9.31	18.49	56.42		14.1	19.10	23.78	38.41	
Netherlands	3.4	12.89	5.93	18.95		13.9	15.75	19.95	25.43	
Switzerland	3.6	3.84	10.55	18.22		9.9	10.33	10.78	12.65	
Canada	137.0	97.20	126.35	97.50		4.3	4.77	8.69	13.39	
Sweden	4.8	4.66	13.98	13.69		5.2	7.69	12.19	15.12	
Australia	97.0	202.06	152.82	167.76	112.0	11.0	14.78	22.85	26.84	28.0
Ceylon	28.0	21.13	25.60	36.12		8.6	29.01	42.90	23.91	
Hong Kong	14.9	12.24	10.48	12.56	11.2	212.3	260.21	344.75	406.31	484.4
Pakistan	1.6	12.90	14.83	43.35		4.2	5.89	16.26	18.40	
Japan	38.5	62.42	152.75	245.04	313.6	46.0	74.61	157.76	224.71	305.2
Malaya-Singapore	0.7	5.40	0.34	7.33		65.9	94.04	98.84	106.39	

*SOURCE: Far Eastern Economic Review Year Book 1966, 1967.

TABLE VI

China's Food Grain Production in Millions of Metric Tons, as Estimated by Experts in Hong Kong

(Since 1957, no firm Chinese government figures have been published.)

1953-57 average	163
1958	193.5
1959	168
1960	160
1961	167
1962	182
1963	179
1964	185
1965	180
1966	175

The major factors underlying the decline in grain production are discussed in Chapter VIII. An additional factor was the introduction of rice double cropping in Hunan, Anhwei and Kwangsi provinces without provisions for extra amounts of water, fertilizer and labor needed to make double cropping worthwhile.

APPENDIX II

CHINA'S INDUSTRIAL CAPACITY

The following run-down on China's industrial plant and its prospects for future expansion is based on the best information published by the government in Peking as screened and supplemented by the China-watchers in Hong Kong. These experts analyze published material in the context of eyewitness accounts by travelers and refugees and by studying the quantity and quality of Chinese exports which pass through Hong Kong.

STEEL. During Japan's occupation of Manchuria, 1931-1945, a substantial steel industry was built there by Chinese workers and technicians, but under the supervision and control of the Japanese. In its peak production year, 1943, this complex turned out a million tons of ingots— 95 per cent of China's production. By 1949, however, due to Russian dismantling and the disorders of civil war, this figure had fallen to 162,000 tons. During the decade after liberation, this Anshan complex was rebuilt, and by 1958, it had 10 blast furnaces, 3 open-hearth shops and was making about 5 million tons of steel yearly. Production fell during the next several years but is now about 5 to 6 million tons annually.

The next largest plant is at Wuhan and was built by the Russians, starting in 1956. Designed for a 3-million-ton ingot capacity to be reached in 1962, experts believe that by 1966, 2 million tons may have been realized. It has 2 blast furnaces, 4 open-hearth shops and assorted finishing mills.

Paotow, in Inner Mongolia, is almost identical to Wuhan in design and was begun at the same time, but neither construction nor production proceeded as rapidly. It was producing only 200,000 ingot tons from one open hearth in 1964. Another was put in operation in 1965. But 1966 production was probably not more than half a million tons.

Other plants at Chungking, Shanghai, Peking, Chengchow, Tientsin, Taiyuan and Penhsihu may produce another 2 or 3 million tons a year, bringing the 1966 production for all of China up to 10 to 12 million tons. While that is nearly twice India's production, it is sufficient to fill only a fraction of China's need for steel, the primary prerequisite for the construction of other industries and the creation of needed infrastructure—roads, bridges, dams, ports and canals.

COAL. Having doubled production from 1956 until 1960, China became the world's largest producer after the United States and the Soviet Union. Production in 1966 was about 250 million tons, of which almost 30 per cent was used in metallurgy, about 20 per cent for power production and about 15 per cent burned in the country's locomotives. Thanks to China's immense reserves, production will probably increase and may reach the 1960 target of 425 million tons some time within the next decade.

PETROLEUM. Long thought to be lacking sufficient oil reserves, China has found deposits which experts think sufficient to sustain a production of 20 to 40 million tons a year. Actual production in 1966 was probably about 10 million tons, and a bottleneck in refining has forced the Chinese to continue importing gasoline, which is likely to remain in short supply for a long time.

NON-FERROUS METALS. China produces enough tin, antimony, mercury, bismuth, tungsten and manganese to export substantial quantities, mostly in the form of concentrates. Copper, aluminum, lead and zinc are produced

147

but not in quantities large enough to meet domestic demands. In all of these metals, and particularly in tin and aluminum, China's reserves are impressive. With the necessary effort and development capital, these reserves could become the base of major domestic and export industries. Lack of capital and technology will probably prevent this from occurring in the immediate future.

CEMENT. Production in 1966 was probably about 10 million tons, not nearly enough to fill the country's growth needs.

CHEMICAL FERTILIZER. The Chinese claimed production of 9 million tons of chemical fertilizer in 1966—one of the few production claims made since 1960. Hong Kong experts put the figure at 6 million gross tons. In nutrient content, this works out to a bit more than 1 million tons and compares favorably to India's half-million ton production. It is estimated that China's production currently is only one-thirtieth of what would be needed to bring China's fertilizer use and yields up to the level of Japan's.

MACHINE BUILDING. China has begun to make machine-tools, engines, trucks and automobiles. These items have been displayed at industrial fairs in Poznan, in Leipzig, in Rumania and in Casa Blanca. The Red Flag sedan, the Red Guard 3.5-ton truck, several other models of trucks, and a large assortment of lathes, milling machines, punch presses and other machines of not very modern design have been widely and proudly displayed by China in many countries. Unfortunately, no Chinese production claims have been made, nor have the Hong Kong experts offered any estimates. One can only conclude that the Chinese have begun producing machines, but they feel that quantity and quality still do not permit direct comparison with other countries.

APPENDIX III

A Prologue to a Poem. From the Cycle "Walkie-Talkie" by Andrei Voznesensky. (Printed in Russian in "Literaturnaya Rossiya," No. 13, for March 24, 1967. Translated by John Scott with help from Robert Magidoff and Maria D. Scott):

I, your dog, oh Epoch,
     am calling on the sleepy authorities—
I feel the coming of Kuchum.*
I feel the mail shirt
     through all the nonsense talk about military communes

I feel Kuchum.
I feel urine
     on the Louvre's pearls
I feel Kuchum.
Dust rises over the horde
     under the mushroom cloud
Men, tear yourselves away
     from your young loved ones,
I feel Kuchum.

*Kuchum—the last of the Siberian Mongol Khans, who tried to reassert the "Golden Horde's" control over Russia, and was finally defeated by Cossack Ottoman Yermak at the end of the sixteenth century.

Listen. It is beginning.
>   The high-cheeked cook
>   is cutting the brain out of a dog,
>   alive and whining,
>   while its long-eared brother
>   is graying with madness—
I feel the coming of the age of Kuchum . . .

Could it be that tomorrow
>   Cosmonauts will return from Mars only to find bar-
>   barian horsemen in charge?
Could it be that Shakespeare
>   will be forced to confess ignorance of "isms"?
Could it be that Stravinski,
>   a garbage pail over his head,
>   will be dragged along howling streets?

I ponder . . .
I pose the question: Is the majority always right?
>   Is the flood in Florence right
>   when it crushes palaces like walnuts?
But in the end, the brain wins, not numbers.
I ponder . . .
The crowd or the individual?
What is longer lasting, a century,
>   or a moment of Michelangelo?
The century is gone, but the moment lasts.

I ponder . . .
The epochal boor, steeped in conformity,
>   will seep over the hills . . .
>   Over our guts, the brute,
The brute measuring little iron heels
>   to new little boots, the boor,
The shadow of a horse
>   dragging slaves on a chain,
Bloodthirsty rockets on TV screens,
>   Boor.
Barn rats gnaw into Marx,
Wrecking the Communist Party,
>   paving the way for the boor party, Brrr . . .
Genghis-Khanism rising
>   like dough in a kneading trough,

Beat it, witchery, or is it only a nightmare?
Beat it!

Madonna on an ikon,
    glittering on a white wall like a woman selling movie
    tickets
    through a moon-shaped glass window,
Please sell me a ticket
    for a show for children only.
It is beyond my strength and comprehension—
    all that's going on . . .
People are never Kuchums . . .
    Kuchums are Godlets, would-be Godlets . . .
    Kuchums are not a nationality . . .
What talk of nationality,
    or of skin color?
We have known blond "supermen"
    who skinned babies for lampshades . . .
The super-East is dreaming about the super-West
    Kuchumism—flood of owlish chauvinism.
    Kuchumism is war . . .

Paris must not be allowed to flame
    like moth over candle
    (What price centuries of history—
    to be again on hands and knees?)
What has revisionism to do with bigots in yurts . . .
    (I hear: "Give us Caspian caviar and the Baikal!")
Will we once more have to carry
    the planet on our backs?

Time.
Pray to Russia
    for its awful fate!
For our selflessness,
    eternal like the sky.
The bullets aimed at Rome,
    at Vienna—into our guts!

Russia—Savior—from whatever Khans!
Eternal Russia!

Again Russia!
    Eternal Russia!

Russia—with open palm—
    Novgorod, open under the sky,
    burns on the plowed plane—
    Like sugar to a horse to the evil Khans
    . . . who whimper . . .

Mother, my Russia
    Don't let yourself be crushed.

A passer-by, I watch haystacks at night
    Covered against the rain.

And so now,
    under the cold cosmic drizzle
    The Earth covers its shoulders with Russia and
    shivers.

BIOGRAPHICAL
SKETCHES OF
PROMINENT CHINESE

CHEN PO-TA: In the past, few people ever heard of Chen Po-ta, Chief Editor of *Hung Chi* (Red Flag), theoretical journal of the Chinese Communist Party.

Today, he is one of the brightest rising stars in the Chinese Communist constellation. When the Party's Central Committee launched the Red Guard movement in August, 1966, as an instrument for the purge of Mao Tse-tung's opposition, Chen was appointed "leader of the group in charge of the Cultural Revolution."

In this new capacity, he has been entrusted with the day-to-day responsibility for the nationwide liquidation of anti-Mao elements.

Chen Po-ta was born in 1904 in Fukien province in East China. At one time he was Chairman Mao's political secretary and ghostwriter.

CHEN YI: One of Red China's political figures well-known in the West is "Marshal" Chen Yi, Peking's Foreign Minister.

Son of a magistrate and born in 1901 in Szechuan province, Chen Yi was well versed in Chinese classics. In 1918, he went to France on a scholarship and later, together with Prime Minister Chou En-lai, stayed on as a Chinese worker-student. After his return to China, he started his varied career as an assistant to a War Lord, then as a newspaper publisher and student of European literature in Peking.

He cooperated with the Nationalists for a while, but in 1928 joined Mao Tse-tung in the latter's Soviet base in Kiangsi province.

As China's Foreign Minister since 1958, Chen Yi has visited many foreign countries in Asia and Africa. He speaks French and likes to write poetry during his leisure moments.

CHIANG CHING: Chiang Ching has become Red China's most famous woman. She is the wife of Chairman Mao Tse-tung and is also his political helpmate.

Over 50 years old, Chiang Ching stepped into the limelight in August, 1966, after some 25 years of domesticity, when her husband launched the Red Guard movement early in the Cultural Revolution.

Today, as first deputy leader of the Central Cultural Revolution Group and adviser to the army's Cultural Revolution Committee, she wields tremendous influence in China's affairs of state.

She has distinguished herself in the "revolutionization" of Chinese literature and art, particularly in the field of centuries-old Peking opera.

Chiang Ching was born into a poor family in a tiny town in Shantung province, North China, between 1910 and 1915; her exact birthdate is unknown. Her early life was known to be avant-garde. Before becoming the present Madame Mao, she was a minor stage and movie actress in Shanghai in the early 1930s. She married Mao in 1941 in the caves of Yenan, the famous wartime base of the Chinese Communists, and bore him two daughters.

At the end of 1968 she ranked sixth in the hierarchy of the Peking regime, after Chairman Mao, Vice Chairman Lin Piao, Premier Chou En-lai, Cultural Revolution leader Chen Po-ta and Politburoman Kang Sheng.

CHIANG CHING-KUO: The eldest son of President Chiang Kai-shek, Ching-Kuo is Minister of Defense of the Republic of China at Taiwan (Formosa Island). He is generally regarded as the heir-apparent to President Chiang and wields great influence in the Nationalist government. He holds the military title of General.

Ching-kuo was born in Chekiang province on March

18, 1910. He received his education at Sun Yat-sen University in Moscow.

Since 1952, he has been a member of the Central Committee of the Chinese Nationalist Party (Kuomintang). He has visited the United States several times. He is married to a Russian and has three sons and a daughter.

CHIANG KAI-SHEK: Chiang is General and President of the Government of the Republic of China in Taiwan (Formosa Island).

Educated at Paoting Military Academy (then the leading school for training army officers) and later in Japan, Chiang led the Northern Expedition of 1927 against the War Lords. In the same year, he was converted to Christianity as a Methodist.

Since the 1930's, his national policies have clashed with the Chinese Communists. In the civil war following World War II, he was driven from the Chinese mainland by Mao Tse-tung's armies.

He is eighty-one years old but still enjoys good health.

CHOU EN-LAI: Prime Minister of the Peking regime. Chou, seventy, is well versed in the Chinese classics and is well traveled in Afro-Asian and Eastern European countries. Educated partly in France, he is doubtless the best-known politician abroad after Chairman Mao.

Chou is a shrewd, persistent political bargainer who believes in the Communist dictum, "the end justifies the means." He is known as the "Mikoyan of China," invariably emerging triumphant from a political or national crisis.

Of literary background, he was born in 1899 in Chekiang province, in Central China.

CHOU YANG: Among high-ranking officials of the Peking regime, Chou Yang was one of the early victims of the "great proletarian Cultural Revolution."

Before his ouster, Chou was Vice Minister of Culture. He was purged by the leading Mao-Lin faction in August, 1966, on grounds of being "anti-revolutionary" and "revisionist."

Chou was born in Hunan province in 1908. He was educated at the University of Shanghai and later went to Japan for further studies.

CHU TEH: This veteran Communist fighter is over eighty-two years old, but he still finds himself at the "Party's Center," being a Vice Chairman of the Communist Party's Central Committee and a member of the Politburo's Standing Committee.

Before the abolition of military ranks in June, 1965, he was known as "Marshal" Chu Teh.

He was born in 1886 in Szechuan province into a rich family and was educated at Yunnan Military Academy.

HSIEH FU-CHIH: As Peking's secret police chief, he is one of the most elusive and mystifying political figures in Mainland China. Reports of his place and date of birth vary from Hupeh to Hunan provinces and from 1897 to 1908, and little is known about his early life.

In 1954, Hsieh was appointed commander and concurrently political commissar of the military region of Kunming, capital of southwestern Yunnan province. The following year he became the boss of the Communist Party's Yunnan Provincial Committee, and a member of the Party's Central Committee in 1956.

Hsieh achieved national stature when he was appointed a Vice Premier of the State Council and member of the National Defense Council in 1965. When the Peking Revolutionary Committee was formed on April 20, 1967, he was chosen by Chairman Mao to become its leader.

Shortly afterward, he was identified also as the political commissar of the Peking Military Region and a member of the Standing Committee of the Military Affairs Commission.

Today he ranks seventh in the Chinese Communist Party hierarchy.

KANG SHENG: Kang Sheng was confirmed a member of the all-important Standing Committee of the Politburo during the Chinese Communist Party's Central Committee plenum in August, 1966. He probably ranks fifth in the hierarchy, after Chairman Mao, Defense Minister Lin

Piao, Prime Minister Chou En-lai, and Cultural Revolution Subcommittee leader Chen Po-ta.

He is believed to be an "expert on peasant problems." In the West, however, he is better known as a leader who often comes in contact with Communist parties of various countries. It is assumed that he is Head of the International Liaison Department of the Party's Central Committee.

Born about 1899 into a wealthy family in Shantung province, Kang studied at the University of Shanghai and joined the Chinese Communist Party in 1925.

KAO KANG: During the early days of the People's Republic of China, Kao Kang was a top Communist leader in the vital region of Manchuria. He was also a member of the Politburo and Head of the State Planning Commission.

At that time, the Peking regime was engaged in political consolidation, and during the "unity campaign," Kao was purged on charges of factionalism. He disappeared completely from public life in the early part of 1954.

Kao's ouster was confirmed publicly after the Party held its conference in March, 1955. He later committed suicide.

LIN PIAO: From the start of the Cultural Revolution in November, 1965, Lin Piao has emerged as the acknowledged Number Two leader after Chairman Mao Tsetung.

As Red China's Minister of National Defense, he is the leading practitioner of Mao's doctrine that claims "All political power grows out of the barrel of a gun" and "The gun must never be allowed to command the Party."

Even if he shows no ambition to step into Mao's shoes, Lin Piao, sixty-one, is in a powerful position, being able to throw his support behind whomever he wishes as Mao's successor. For behind him stands the 2.7 million men of the People's Liberation Army.

LIU SHAO-CHI: As the prime target of Mao's Cultural Revolution, President Liu Shao-chi's political career came to an end in October of 1968 when an enlarged plenum of the Central Committee under Mao's chairmanship fired him from all his jobs and expelled him from the Party as a traitor and a counter-revolutionary.

After having been labeled "number one capitalist-roader" and "China's Khrushchev" for the previous three years, he was officially and directly denounced by name as "a renegade, traitor and scab hiding in the Party, and a running-dog of imperialism, modern revisionism and Kuomintang reactionaries." Liu was thrown out in absentia, without the right of self-defense.

The ascetic elder statesman was born in 1898 to a small landowner family in Hunan province. He has known his fellow-provincial Mao from their high-school days and collaborated with him for the cause of Chinese communism during the past four decades.

Liu's present fate is uncertain.

MAO TSE-TUNG: Chairman of the Chinese Communist Party and ruler of the 700 million Chinese on the Mainland, Mao is old and infirm at seventy-five. He fears that "Khrushchevian revisionism" or "Western capitalism" may emerge in China after his death.

To perpetuate "Maoism," he has launched the Cultural Revolution designed to purge all opposition to the "thought of Mao Tse-tung," thereby producing a serious upheaval in Mainland China. Chairman Mao's campaign is meeting with stiff resistance from his party colleagues, including Chief of State Liu Shao-chi and Secretary General Teng Hsiao-ping.

Mao Tse-tung was born on December 26, 1893, in Hunan province, Central China.

PENG CHEN: The former Mayor of Peking and First Secretary of the Peking Party Committee, Peng Chen was the first top-ranking leader to fall victim to Mao Tse-tung's Cultural Revolution.

When he was purged on grounds of "anti-Party, anti-Socialist" activities in June, 1966, Peng was a member of the Politburo, Secretariat and Central Committee of the Chinese Communist Party. He was also Vice Chairman and Secretary General of the Standing Committee of the National People's Congress.

A lively, quick-witted and smiling politician, Peng was born to poor parents in 1899 in Shansi province, North China. He joined the Chinese Communist Party in the early 1920s and started his political career as a labor organizer and agitator.

PENG TE-HUAI: After his dismissal as Minister of National Defense by Chairman Mao in 1959, "Marshal" Peng Te-huai has been rarely heard of.

Before his purge, he was second only to Chu Teh in Red China's military affairs. He was born of wealthy parents in 1900 in Hunan province.

There was no official public explanation for Peng's ouster in 1959, but it was generally believed that he opposed Mao's "people's commune" and hard-line policy toward Soviet Russia. He was replaced by Lin Piao.

In early 1967, as the power struggle was spreading throughout Mainland China, Peng was reported arrested by the authorities on vague charges of "anti-party" activities. His fate is unknown.

PO I-PO: When the Chinese Communists established their regime in Peking in 1949, Po I-po was its first Minister of Finance.

When Red China launched its first Five-Year Plan in 1952, Po joined the State Planning Commission, set up in November of the same year, and relinquished the Minister of Finance portfolio the next year.

As Peking's leading economic planner, Po has been largely responsible for the country's implementation of the economic policies.

Po was purged by the Mao-Lin faction in the struggle for power in Mainland China in 1966. According to wall posters in Peking, Po is reported to have tried suicide but without success.

Po was born in 1907 in Shansi province.

SOONG CHING LING: She is the famous Madame Sun, widow of Dr. Sun Yat-sen. Because of differences of opinion with her brother-in-law, President Chiang Kai-shek of the Nationalist Chinese government, she joined a leftwing group at Hankow and later worked for the Chinese Communists.

She is now a Vice Chairman of the Peking regime, a Deputy for Shanghai to the National People's Congress and Chairman of the Sino-Soviet Friendship Association.

Born in 1890, Ching-ling is the second daughter of an influential, wealthy Shanghai businessman and missionary, Charles Jones Soong. She was educated at Wesleyan College in Connecticut. She became associated with Dr. Sun in 1912, who was then engaged in revolutionary activity and married him in 1915 during his political exile in Japan.

SOONG MEI-LING: In America, where she was educated at Wellesley College, she is better known as Mayling Soong.

Born on April 1, 1901, into a wealthy businessman's family, Mayling is the youngest of the three famous "Soong sisters," the other two being Soong Ching-ling (Madame Sun Yat-sen) and Soong Ai-ling (Madame H. H. Kung).

The beautiful and talented Mayling was married to President Chiang Kai-shek on December 1, 1927. She has had great influence over President Chiang's career and has served as an important link for him with the West.

SUN YAT-SEN: A medical doctor by training, Dr. Sun is generally accepted by the Chinese all over the world as the "Father of the Chinese Republic." He is revered both in Communist China and Nationalist China as the leader who led the overthrow of the Manchu Dynasty.

He was the founder of "Tung Meng Hui," forerunner of the future Nationalist Party (Kuomintang).

He was born November 12, 1866, in Chungshan, Kwangtung province. He received his early education at the Anglican Mission School and later attended Hawaii College in Honolulu.

He died in Peking on March 12, 1925.

TAO CHU: The meteroric rise of Tao Chu to membership in the Standing Committee of the Politburo in mid-

August, 1966, was as bewildering as his sudden fall into disfavor in early 1967.

As a protégé of Defense Minister Lin Piao, Tao was appointed Chief of the Propaganda Department of the Party's Central Committee in the fall of 1966, replacing the purged Lu Ting-yi.

However, shortly afterward he became a target for attacks by "revolutionary rebels" who charged him with revisionism.

Tao had won the praise of the Communist leadership for his work in the Party's Central South Bureau, of which he was First Secretary, with Kwangtung province as his base. He was appointed a Vice Premier in early 1965.

Tao Chu was born in Hunan province in 1906.

TENG HSIAO-PING: In the current power struggle in Mainland China, this little and peppery General Secretary of the Chinese Communist Party's Central Committee is being attacked by the Mao-Lin faction.

Teng was born in 1904 in Szechuan province.

Teng has been General Secretary of the Party since 1954. As such, he reports to the Party on major political matters. He became a member of the Politburo's Standing Committee in 1956.

Pro-Mao elements have charged Teng with being a "power holder who takes the capitalist road." Wall posters in Peking in early 1967 said that Teng confessed his "erroneous line." Whether this is true or not remains to be seen.

YAO WEN-YUAN: Yao is the bright young man among Peking's aging top leadership. Barely forty years old, he was Chairman Mao's confidant and ideologist in the Mao-Liu power struggle. He is also a leading member of the Central Cultural Revolution Group.

Little is known about his youth, except that he lived in Shanghai where he was well known as a rather prolific writer.

Yao is the author of the much-publicized article in which he denounced the anti-Mao allegorical novel entitled *Hai Jui Dismissed from Office* written by Professor

Wu Han. His critique was publicized in *Wen Hui Pao*, the Maoist daily in Shanghai, on November 10, 1965. It was officially described as "the signal for the counter-offensive in full force by the proletariat against the reactionary bourgeoisie."

Yao was thus regarded as the vanguard who fired the first shot in Mao's Cultural Revolution. According to report, he wrote the article at the "request" of Chairman Mao and under the "direct guidance" of Madame Mao.

In August, 1968, when Mao decided to bring the leading role of the working class into full play at the expense of the bungling Red Guards, it was again Yao who was entrusted with the task of writing the major policy article entitled "The Working Class Must Lead in Everything." The article was published in *Hung Chi* (Red Flag), theoretical journal of the Chinese Communist Party, on August 25, 1968.

BRIEF BIBLIOGRAPHY

BARNETT, A. DOAK, *China on the Eve of Communist Take-over*. Frederick A. Praeger, 1963.* *Communist China and Asia*. Vintage Books, 1961.*

BLUM, ROBERT H., *The U.S. and China-World Affairs*, (Edited by A. Doak Barnett). McGraw Hill, 1966.*

CHIANG KAI-SHEK, *China's Destiny*. Macmillan, 1947. *Soviet Russia in China*. Farrar, Straus and Cudahy, 1957.*

FESSLER, LOREN, *China-Life World Library*. Time Inc., 1963.

LI, DUN J., *The Ageless China*. Charles Scribner & Sons, 1965.*

MACFAQUHAR, RODERICK, *The Hundred Flowers Campaign and the Chinese Intellectuals*. Frederick A. Praeger, 1960.

REISCHAUER, EDWIN O., and FAIRBANK, JOHN K., *East Asia: The Great Tradition*. Houghton Mifflin, 1960.

SCHRAM, STUART, *Mao Tse-tung*. Simon and Schuster, 1967.*

* Available in paperback.

SCHWARTZ, BENJAMIN, *Chinese Communism and the Rise of Mao*. Howard University Press, 1951.*

SCOTT, JOHN, *Crisis in Communist China*. Time Inc., 1962.

SNOW, EDGAR, *Red Star Over China*. Modern Library, 1944.* *The Other Side of the River*. Random House, 1962.

WALEY, ARTHUR, *The Life and Times of Po Chu'i*. Macmillan, 1949. *The Poetry and Career of Li Po*. Macmillan, 1950. *Yuan Mei: Eighteenth Century Chinese Poet*. Evergreen Book, 1958. Trans. of *The Book of Songs*. Evergreen Book, 1960.*

* Available in paperback.

INDEX

AFGHANISTAN, 31, 36, 80, 97
Africa, China's influence, 69, 84–
    85, 91, 96–98
Agriculture, 25, 26, 30–32, 38, 43,
    135
  capital investment, 60
  collectivization, 59–60
  effect of Great Leap, 69–71
  fertilizer shortage, 61, 66
  Great Retreat, 69–70
  industrial slowdown in favor
    of, 73–76
  kitchen gardens, 70, 101, 118
  Nationalist China, 110–111
  production, 57–58, 60, 66–68,
    drop in, 38, 66, 68, 82
    mid-60s, 101–102, 128
  reforms, 42, 56–57
Air force, 105–106
Air transportation, 103
Albania, 96–98
Anhwei province, 126
Arab states, 35, 91
Archeological background, 25
Armed forces, 105–107, 118
  military equipment, 34, 102,
    105–106
  role in Great Leap, 65, 67
Arts and artists, 34, 36
Asia, China's influence, 69, 84–
    85, 91, 96, 98
Atomic program, 76, 102, 104,
    106
  Soviet promises of aid, 62, 69
Australia, China's trade with,
    75–76, 94, 103
Automobile and truck produc-
    tion, 60–61, 66, 79, 102,
    147

BANDUNG CONFERENCE, 93, 98

Barbarian invasions, 30–35
"Better Red than Expert," 121,
    130
Birth control, 63, 99–101
Blukher, Marshal Vasili, 21
Borodin, Mikhail, 21, 48, 49, 83
Boxer Rebellion, 44
Brainwashing and thought con-
    trol, 58, 61
Browder, Earl, 83
Buddhism, 28–29, 87
Burma, 29, 35, 36, 38, 40, 80,
    105, 113, 116
  relations with China, 91, 92–
    93, 97
Businessmen, Communist treat-
    ment of, 57–58

CAIRO DECLARATION, 92
Cambodia, 29, 83, 97, 103, 113
Canada, China's trade with, 75–
    76, 94, 103
Canal system, 35, 38–39, 64, 70
Canton, China, 40, 83, 124–125
Capitalism, 119
Cement production, 60, 72, 74,
    147
Ceylon, 29, 97
Chandrasekhar, S., 64, 66
Chang Lin-chih, 21
Character, Chinese, 36, 39, 46
Chen Po-ta, 122, 152–153, 156
Chen Yi (Foreign Minister),
    79, 127, 152–153
Chen Yun (Vice President), 61
Chen Ch'eng-kung, 37
Chiang-Ching (Mao's wife), 52,
    122, 126
Chiang Ching-kuo (son of
    Chiang Kai-shek), 109–
    110, 112, 152

165

Chiang Kai-shek, 45–46, 48, 84, 92, 108–110, 112–113, 154, 158–159
  attack on Communists, 49, 51–53
  kidnapped, 52
  withdrawal to Taiwan, 55
Children, 100
  in the communes, 64–65, 70
Ch'in rulers, 30–31
China, 38
  future trends, 129–137
  isolation and encirclement, 135
  origin of name, 30
  size of, 38
"China Lobby," 136
China News Service, 96
Chinese Communist Party, 22, 45, 134
  Central Committee, 73, 120–123
  conflict with Soviets; see Sino-Soviet conflict
  criticism of, 61
  discipline of, 55
  execution of opposition, 57
  formation of, 47–48
  leadership, 61, 119, 131–132, 152–160
  Long March, 51–52
  Mao, leader of, 51–52
  members, 51
  Moscow's attempts to control, 47–48, 77–78, 83–84
  organization of, 83
  purge by Chiang Kai-shek, 49, 51–53
  rectification campaign, 61
  revisionists, 87, 118–120
  Seventh Congress, 53
  United Front period, 53
  victory in 1949, 81, 110
Chinese Red Army, 22
Chinese Soviet Republic, 51, 84
Ch'ing Dynasty, 37
Chou Dynasty, 26–30
  poets, 29–30
Chou En-lai (Premier), 48, 51, 61–62, 67–68, 153–156
  on communes, 63
  and Cultural Revolution, 127
  Soviet relations and, 77, 84
  travels, 92–93
  on United Nations, 130

Chou Yang, 153–154
Christianity, 37, 42, 44
  Communism and, 87–89
Chu Teh, 48–49, 51, 77, 84, 155
Chu Yuan-chang, 35
Chuang Tzu (poet), 30
Civil service system, 31, 35
Civil war, 21–23, 46, 112–113, 133
Civilization, Chinese, 25–26, 32
Class struggle, 21, 119–120
Cleanliness campaign, 119
Coal production, 56, 60, 66, 72–73, 83, 94, 102, 146
Collectivization, 59–60
Colleges and universities, 66, 121, 123–124
COMECON (Council for Mutual Economic Aid), 81
Comintern, 47–48, 83
Communes, 62–65
  children, 64
  dissolution of, 67–70, 90, 101
  mobilization of peasants, 63–65, 74–75
  organization of, 64
  secondary projects, 64, 70
  shops and factories, 64
  small garden plots, 70
  Soviet reaction, 69
  workers sent back to villages, 73–74
Communications, 73
Communism, 87–88
  doctrinal principles, 87–88
  in underdeveloped countries, 90
Communist Bloc countries, 91, 96
  China's trade with, 103
Communist Party; see Chinese Communist Party
Confucius, 28, 31, 87
  influence of, 28
  teachings of, 28–29, 33, 36
Consumer goods, 61
Cooperatives, 118
Cotton, 68
Cuba, 97
Cultural Revolution, 22, 52, 87, 94, 98, 118–128
  attack on intellectuals, 119–120
  economic effects, 126–127
  Red Guards, 122–127; see also Red Guards

schools closed, 121–122, 126
sixteen-point decision, 122
Culture, Chinese, 32, 39, 46

DAIREN, 59, 85
de Gaulle, Charles, 92
Denmark, 91
Developing countries, China's influence, 96–98
Dictionaries, 38, 104
Diseases, 128, 132

ECONOMY, CHINA, 60, 99–107
agriculture, 101
armed forces, 105–106
effect of Great Retreat, 76
Gross National Product, 79, 106–107
industry, 102
Nationalist China, 109–112, 133
nuclear weapons, 106
productive forces, 79–80
rationing, 73, 76, 103
recovery from Great Leap, 59, 76, 118
Sino-Soviet conflict and, 79–82
trade, 103
Education, 43, 61, 104–105, 121
language problem, 104–105
schools closed, 121–122, 127
on Taiwan, 111
Egyptian civilization, 25–26, 38
Electric power, 56, 60, 102
Taiwan, 111
Empress Dowager, 43–44
Exports and imports, 75–76, 82, 101, 103, 111

FAMILY LIFE, 39, 70–72
Fertilizers, 70, 101, 132, 147
chemical plans, 73, 76, 94, 101
Feudal states, 27, 30
Five-Year Plan, 72
Floods and famines, 26, 32, 36, 38, 42
Food shortages, 38, 62, 66–68, 79–80, 132
grain imports, 76, 94, 101
production, 39, 94, 101, 103
rationing, 73, 76, 103

Foot binding, 33–34
Foreign aid program, 82–83, 96–97, 119, 130
Foreign exchange reserves, 76, 81
Foreign relations, 91–98
developing nations, 96–98
economic aid, 96–97
future trends, 118–119, 129–131
isolation from Soviets, 98
Foreigners, 35, 40, 43
concessions sought by, 43, 45
confiscation of property, 57
exclusion of, 37, 40, 43
Forests, 38, 80
Formosa; see Taiwan
Formosa Strait, 109
Fragmentation, 23
French colonization, 43, 47, 92
Fukien province, 109, 127

GENEVA CONFERENCES, 93, 95
George, Henry, 44
George III, King of England, 40
German colonization, 43, 47
Ghana, 97
Ghengis Khan, 34
Girls, treatment of, 33
Gobi desert, 106
Gold reserves, 56, 103
Gordon, Charles, 42
Graft and corruption, 41–42, 118–119
Grain, 101, 132–133
imports of, 76, 94, 101
Great Britain, 40–43, 91
"Great Leap," 62, 90, 100–101, 103
communes, 62–65
effect on armed forces, 65–67
effect on education, 66
Soviet reaction, 69
targets and false statistics, 65–66
"Great Retreat," 69
effect on industry, 73–76
effect on trade, 75–76
Great Wall of China, 30, 34, 78
Greater East Asia Co-Prosperity Sphere, 46
Gross National Product (GNP), 79, 107
Nationalist China, 110

Guerrilla warfare, 49, 50–51, 93

HAN DYNASTY, 31, 78
Harbin, 78, 124
Hemp, 25
History of China, 21–22, 25–39
  archeological beginnings, 25–26
  Ch'ing Dynasty, 37
  Chou Dynasty, 26–30
  Marxist analyses of, 21–22
  rewriting of, 31
  T'ai P'ing Rebellion, 42
Hong Kong, 41–43, 58, 113–116
  anti-British riots, 115
  China's trade with, 103
  China-watchers, 13, 126, 145
  government, 114
  industries, 113–114
  Overseas Chinese, 113–115
  relations with Mainland, 115
  sources of funds for China, 94, 115
Horses, 34
Hospitals, 45
Hsia Dynasty, 26
Hsieh, S. T., 15
Hu Yao-pang, 122
Hunan province, 49, 51
Hung Chi see Red Flag
Hung Hsiu-ch'uan, 42
Hungary, 86, 97
Hunger, problem of, 36, 38, 51, 68, 75–76, 79–80, 132–133
Hydrogen bomb, 106

IDEOGRAPHS, 31, 104
Illiteracy, 38, 59
India, 22–23, 35–36, 80, 91–92, 134
  China's invasion of, 93–94, 97–98, 130
Indian Ocean, 31, 35
Indo-Chinese war, 93
Indonesia, 35, 91–92, 97–98
  defeat of Communists, 98
  Overseas Chinese, 116–117
Industrial production, 43, 56–58, 60, 102–103, 129–130, 145–147
  capital investments, 60, 132
  effect of Great Leap, 72–74
  effect of Great Retreat, 73–76
  falsification of statistics, 66

  future trends, 132–133
  heavy industry, 60, 75
  reduction of targets, 67–68, 73–76
  Soviet aid, 60
  Taiwan, 110–111
  use of armed forces, 65
Industrialization, socialist, 59
  communes, 62–65
Inner Mongolia, 127, 134
Intellectuals, 43, 48, 56, 61, 66, 90, 118, 131
  purge of, 119–120
Inventions, 31, 39
Investment capital, need for, 60, 132
Iran, 88
Iraq, 38
Iron and steel production, 27, 56, 60, 68, 72, 94, 102, 145–146
  backyard blast furnaces, 64, 68
  downward revision, 68
  falsification of statistics, 66
Irrigation system, 38
Islam religion, 87–88

JADE AND IVORY, 26, 36
Japan, 36, 43, 113
  China's trade with, 81–82, 93–94, 103
  industrial revolution, 133
  invasion of China, 46, 52–53
  occupation of Korea, 43, 108
  occupation of Manchuria, 43, 46, 53
  relations with China, 91, 93
  relations with Soviets, 89

KANG SHENG, 155–156
Kao Kang, 156
Kazakhstan, 31, 78, 89
Khalkhagol, Mongolia, 89
Kharbin, 79
Khrushchev, Nikita, 59, 77, 85–87
  revisionism, 119
Kiangsi province, 49, 51, 84
Kiangsu province, 126
Korea, 31, 35–36, 80
  Japanese occupation, 43, 108
Korean War, 58–59, 92–93, 110, 136

Koxinga (Ming general), 37–38
Kuang Hsu, Emperor, 43
Kublai Khan, 35
Kuo Mo-jo (Intellectual leader), 94
Kuomintang or "National People's Party" (KMT), 45, 83–84, 159
  Communist Party and, 48–49, 83
Kwangtung province, 22

LAN P'ING (Mao's wife), 52
Lanchow (nuclear installation), 106, 135
Land reform, 31, 45, 50, 56–57, 59
  Nationalist China, 108–109
Languages, Chinese, 31, 40, 60–61, 104–105
Lao Tzu, 27–28
Laos, 80, 105
Latin America, 91, 97–98
Lee Kuan Yew, 116
Legends and sagas, 25–26
Lenin, I.V., 47–48, 50, 85
Li Choh-ming, 65
Li Fu-chun (state planning commission), 73–75
Li Po (poet), 32–33
Liao Mo-sha, 120
Liberation Army Daily, 22, 120, 127
Lin Piao, Marshal, 22, 67, 120, 122–123, 125, 127, 155–156, 160
Literature, 27, 32–34, 36
Liu Shao-chi (President), 54, 62–63, 77, 84, 121–123, 156–157
  leader of revisionists, 127, 157
Livestock, 25, 68
  pigs, 73, 101, 118
Lo Jui-ching (army chief of staff), 21, 67
Lominadze, V., 83
Long March, 51–52, 84, 119
Lop Nor, 106, 135
Lu Ping, 120
Lu Ting-yi (minister of culture), 120, 160

MACHINE TOOLS, 60, 72, 151

Mainland China, 15, 21, 55
  intra-party struggles, 89–90
  unification of, 31, 45, 55
Malaya, 91, 93, 113, 117, 132
Malaysia, 35, 116
Manchu Dynasty, 37–39, 78, 159
  overthrow, 45
Manchuria, 78, 89, 134
  armed forces, 105
  coal mines, 72–73
  heavy industry, 45, 145–146
  Japanese occupation, 43, 46, 53
  Soviet invasion of, 43, 53, 56, 59, 80, 85
Manufacturing industries, 102
Mao Tse-tung, 22, 47–55, 156–157
  Chiang Kai-shek and, 51
  Chinese Soviet Republic, 55, 84
  Communist theoretician, 85
  created Asian form of Marxism, 51, 85–86
  cult of, 22, 54, 117
  "eight principles," 66
  errors made by, 131
  family background, 47, 52
  "Great Leap" forward, 62
  leader of Communist Party, 48, 51–52, 54, 83, 85–86
  opposition to Khrushchev, 86
  People's Liberation Army, 52
  Quotations of Chairman Mao, 122
  Red Guards and, 122–126
  resistence against, 51, 121–122, 125–126
  resumes civil war, 54
  revolutionary tactics, 37, 47–50, 57–58, 85
  "socialist education" movement, 119
  Soviet Union and, 48–49, 77, 84–86
  swim in Yangtze River, 121
  thoughts of, 50, 53–54, 74, 96, 100, 119–120, 156
  visits to Moscow, 56
  on warfare, 50–51
Marriages, restrictions on, 100
Marx, Karl, 44, 47, 85, 87, 89
  analyses of recent history, 22
Mende, Tibor, 64

Mineral resources, 80, 102, 146–147
Ming Dynasty, 35–37
Minority groups, 99
Missionaries, 37, 43, 45
Modernization, need for, 43
Money and currency, 31, 34
Mongolia, 30–31, 40, 97
Mongols, invasion of China, 34–36
Mukden, 78

NANKING, 42, 124
National budget, 61
National guard, 106
National People's Congress, 61
Nationalist China, 59, 108–113; see also Taiwan
  invasion of Mainland, 129–130, 134–135
  relations with Chinese Communists, 52–54, 91–92
Nationalist Party, 159; see also Kuomintang
Nationalization of industry, 57–58
Navy, China's, 106
Nehru, 92–94
Nepal, 29, 97
North Korea, 96
North Vietnam, 96–97, 103
  Chinese aid to, 130–132
Nuclear test ban treaty, 130
Nuclear weapons, 69, 106–107, 130, 132, 135

"OPEN DOOR POLICY," 43
Opium trade, 41–42
Overseas Chinese, 44, 92, 113–117
  non-assimilation of, 117

PAKISTAN, 97–98, 103
Pan Ku, 26
Panch Shila, 93
Paotow (nuclear installation), 106, 135, 146
Peaceful coexistence, 86–87
Peasants, 118, 130, 132, 135
  effect of "Great Leap" on, 67
  rebellions, 21, 33, 37, 55

Peking, 35, 44
  foreigners in, 43
  Red Guards, 123–125
Peng Chen (Mayor of Peking), 94, 120, 157–158
Peng Te-huai, Marshal, 67, 120, 158
People's Daily, 61–62, 65, 68, 73, 75, 82, 87, 104, 120, 125, 157
People's Liberation Army, 21–22, 52–54, 84, 123, 134, 156
People's Republic of China, 77, 85
  proclaimed by Mao, 55
Pescadores, 43, 108
Petroleum, 102, 146
Philippines, 91, 93, 113, 116
Philosophy, Chinese, 27
  Confucius, 28–30
  Lao Tzu, 27–28, 30
Po I-po, 74, 158
Poets and poetry, 27, 32–34, 90
  Chou Dynasty, 29–30
  "Great Leap," 66
Polo, Marco, 35
Population growth, 37, 39, 46, 79, 99–101, 137
  birth control, 99–101
  future trends, 114
  rate of, 99–101
Port Arthur, 59, 78, 85
Portuguese, at Macao, 37
Posters, wall, 21, 123, 126, 158
Pottery and porcelain, 26, 36, 38, 40
Printing, invention of, 33–34
Prison and labor camps, 58, 61
Propaganda, 58, 61
Prostitution, 119

QUEMOY AND MATSU, 107, 110

RACE RELATIONS, 40, 85
Radio broadcasts, 95
Railroads, 56, 79, 85, 102
  Taiwan, 110–111
Rationing, 73, 76, 103
Raw Materials, 61, 74
Rectification campaign, 61
Red Flag (newspaper), 87, 122, 125, 152, 157

Red Guards, 21–22, 94, 122–128, 131
  army control, 126–127
  blockade of Soviet Embassy, 126
  formation of, 122–123
  mass demonstrations, 122
  leaders, 152
  vandalism and destruction, 123–127
Regionalism, 125
Religion, 37, 42
  and Communism, 87–90
  opposition to, 43–44, 123–124
Republic of China, 44–45, 108–113; see also Taiwan
Revisionism, 118–119, 127–129, 137
  future outlook for, 131–132
  struggle against, 118–120, 122
Revolutionary movements, 44, 58, 68, 87–90, 125
  counter-revolutionary reaction, 57
  dynamics of development, 88–89
  Mao's theories, 37, 47–48, 50, 56–58, 85, 123
  in Oriental lands, 84
  schismatic tendency, 88
Ricci, Matteo (Jesuit missionary), 37
Rice, 82, 110–111, 133
Rivers, 32, 102
Roads and road-building, 35, 56, 64, 102
Rumania, 34
Russia; see also Soviet Union
  invasions from the East, 34–35, 78
  in Manchuria, 43
  relations with China, 43

SCHOOLS, 45, 66–67; see also Education
Science, 31, 39, 60
  education and, 104–105
  nuclear, 106–107
  research and development, 104–105
Secret societies, 43–46
Shang Dynasty, 26–27
Shanghai, 41, 45, 66–67, 83
  Red Guards, 123–124

Shantung province, 28, 127
Shen Chou, 36
Shih Huang Ti, 31
Shih Nai-an (novelist), 34
Ships and shipping, 31, 35, 103
Siberia, 31, 38, 78, 89, 132
Silk industry, 40
Singapore, Overseas Chinese, 113, 116
Sinkiang, 22, 89, 125, 127, 134
Sino-Soviet conflict, 69, 77–90, 129–132
  attacks on each other, 87
  danger of war, 89
  dispute on global strategy, 86–87
  dynamics of schism, 87–90
  economic conflict, 79–83
  historic enmity, 78–79
  ideological differences, 78, 86–90
  Moscow's leadership of world communism, 77
  ouster of Khrushchev, 87
  political disagreements, 83–87
  territorial disputes, 78–79
  Treaty of Friendship and Mutual Assistance, 77–78
Society, Chinese, 36
Somalia, 97
Soong, Charles Jones, 159
Soong, Ching-ling, 45, 158–159
Soong, May-ling, 45, 159
Soong, T.V., 45
South Vietnam, Communist guerrillas, 93
Soviet Union
  Central Asia, 38, 78, 132
  agents in China, 47–48
  aid given Chiang Kai-shek, 45–46, 52–53
  Chinese policy, 48, 54, 69; see also Sino-Soviet conflict
  economic aid to China, 56–57, 59, 62, 80–83
  China's repayment, 101, 103
  refusal to grant debt moratorium, 82
  foreign-language broadcasts, 95
  future role, 134
  Gross National Product, 79
  invasion of Manchuria, 43, 53, 56, 59, 80, 85
  literature, 90

policies in Poland and Hungary, 69
population, 79
reparations program, 80
Stalin purges, 21
technicians in China, 59, 69, 73, 81–82
trade with China, 81–82, 101, 103
Twentieth Congress, 85
Twenty-first Congress, 86
withdrawal of support from China, 69
Stalin, Joseph, 80, 85
Chinese policy, 48–49, 54, 83
death of, 85
de-Stalinization policies, 86–87
purges, 21
Statistics, falsification of, 65–66, 68
Steel production; see Iron and steel production
Strikes, 61
Suharto, General, 116
Sukarno (ex-president), 116
Sun Tsu, 50
Sun Yat-sen, Dr., 44–45, 83, 158–159
Sung Dynasty, 34
Szechuan province, 22, 126

TAIPEI, 108
T'ai P'ing Rebellion, 42–43
Taimat, Goddess of Chaos, 26
Taiwan (Formosa), 37–38, 43, 95–96, 107, 108–113, 132
agriculture, 110–111
army, 109–110
economic development, 108–111, 133–134
education, 111
future of, 112–113
government, 111–112
invasion of Mainland, 109–110, 130, 134–135
Japanese occupation, 108–109
land reform, 109
Nationalist withdrawal to, 55
population, 108, 111
Overseas Chinese and, 117, 136
United Nations membership, 109, 113

United States aid, 54, 109, 133, 136
T'ang Dynasty, 32–33
Tanzania, 88, 97
Tao Chu, 159–160
Taoism, 27–29, 42
Tartars, 34–35, 78
Taxes and taxation, 60
Tea industry, 40
Teng Hsiao-ping, 157, 160
Teng To, 120
Textile industry, 45, 83
Thailand, 29, 35, 91
Tibet, 22, 29, 38, 76, 93, 127, 134
Trade relations, 58, 60–61, 93, 103–104
"Great Retreat," effects of, 75–76
luxury goods, 40
opening of ports, 41–43
opium trade, 41–42
with Soviets, 81–82, 101, 103
Transportation, 60, 65, 73, 102–103
Tu Fu (poet), 32

UNITED NATIONS, 59, 92
China's bid for seat, 96, 130–132, 135–136
Nationalist China and, 91–92, 109, 113
United States, 42, 44, 103–104
Communist China and, 91, 94–95, 98, 135–137
Nationalist China and, 53–55, 109, 136
war with China, chances of, 129, 135–137

VIETNAM, 31, 35, 80, 105–106; see also North Vietnam; and South Vietnam
Overseas Chinese, 113
Vietnam war, 110
Voitinsky, Grigory, 47
Voznesensky, Andrei, 90, 148

"WALK ON TWO LEGS" SLOGAN, 67
Wang En-mao, 125

172

War Lords, 44–45
Ward, Frederick, 42
Wars of national liberation, 119, 130
Warsaw, Poland, diplomatic talks between China and U.S., 95, 136
Water conservation, 65
Weapons and ammunition, 34–35, 105–106
Western powers, 40–46
Women in China, 33–34
Workers, sent back to villages, 73–74, 76
Working classes, 83, 118–119, 131
Wu Han, 120

Wuchang, uprising in, 44
Wuhan, 51, 67, 149

YANG TSU (poet), 29–30
Yangtze River, 26–27, 32, 121
Yellow River, 25, 27, 32
Yemen, 83, 96–97
Yen, C.K., 112
Yenan, 125
    Long March to, 51–52, 84, 119
Yew, Lee Kuan, 116
Yin and Yang, 26
Young Communist League, 122
Yuan Dynasty, 34–35

AMERICA IS GROWING UP WITH AVON BOOKS

THE CAMELOT ![CAMELOT] LINE LEADS THE WAY

ANDERSON, MARIAN
My Lord What a Morning   ZS1290   60¢

BECKHARD, ARTHUR
Albert Einstein   ZG109   50¢

BURLINGAME, ROGER
Scientists Behind the Inventors ZS123   60¢

BUSONI, RAFAELLO
The Man Who Was Don Quixote ZS133   60¢

BYRD, RICHARD E.
Alone   ZS124   60¢

CLARKE, A. C.
The Coast of Coral   ZV125   75¢

DAREFF, HAL
The Story of Vietnam   ZS121   60¢

DURRELL, GERALD
Menagerie Manor   ZS115   60¢

FOLLETT, BARBARA NEWHALL
The House Without Windows   ZS127   60¢

FRIBOURG, MARJORIE
The Supreme Court in American
History   ZV140   75¢

FRIBOURG, MARJORIE
The Bill of Rights   ZN149   95¢